# Preliminaries to Speech Analysis

## The Distinctive Features and their Correlates

Roman Jakobson

C. Gunnar M. Fant

Morris Halle

THE M·I·T PRESS
MASSACHUSETTS INSTITUTE OF TECHNOLOGY
CAMBRIDGE, MASSACHUSETTS

*Sixth Printing, September, 1965*

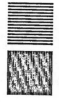

M I T  P r e s s

# 0262600013

JAKOBSON
PRELIMINARIES

Printed In The United States of America

# CONTENTS

# PREFACE

This report proposes some questions to be discussed by specialists working on various aspects of speech communication. These questions concern the ultimate discrete components of language, their specific structure, their inventory in the languages of the world, their identification on the acoustical and perceptual levels and their articulatory prerequisites.

We regard the present list of distinctive features, and particularly their definitions on different levels, as a provisional sketch which is open to discussion and which requires experimental verification and further elaboration. The nature of these problems calls for coordinated research by linguists, psychologists, experts in the physiology of speech and hearing, physicists, communications and electronics engineers, mathematicians, students in symbolic logic and semiotics, and neurologists dealing with language disturbances, as well as the investigators of the poetic use of speech sounds.

The occasional remarks on auditory experience with respect to single distinctive features are meant merely as clues to future experiments in this domain. The articulatory data have deliberately been made brief and their only justification is a desire to outline the connection between the motor means and the acoustic effect; for a more complete treatment of articulatory movements see handbooks of general phonetics (1).

Since this study is addressed to workers in several fields, it was considered appropriate in places, to include certain data even though it might appear elementary to the specialist in any one domain. We have done our utmost to avoid the ambiguity and misunderstanding resulting from the unfortunate diversity of the terminology used in the different disciplines relating to communication.

The names of the distinctive features are meant to denote linguistic discriminations: in other words, the significant discriminations utilized in the code common to the members of a speech community. The stage of the speech event to which a given term is ètymologically connected is much less important. Thus a term which alludes to the articulation may at times be used if the articulatory fact in question is common to all the manifestations of the given feature, e.g., the nasalization feature. Similarly, it is not important whether the term refers primarily to the physical or perceptual level, as long as the feature is definable on both levels. In cases where no generally accepted term was available, we have used names for certain distinctive features which may later be supplanted by more suitable ones. Nevertheless, a discussion of the features themselves seems to us more pertinent than an argument over their labels.

Wherever suitable English examples were available, they have been used. Unless otherwise indicated the specimens are from the stabilized and unified British Standard which has been exhaustively described under the label RP (Received Pronunciation) coined by Daniel Jones (2). When languages other than

English are used, we have endeavored to make the examples as simple and as clear as possible.

The signs employed in transcribed examples are those of the International Phonetic Association (3) with a few modifications. A) The affricates are represented by single letters, the same as those used for the corresponding (homorganic) constrictives but with a superscript $\hat{}$: sh - $/\hat{\int}/$, ch - $/\hat{f}/$. B) When indicating the stress, the sign is placed immediately before the accented vowel. C) In accordance with the proposals of the Copenhagen Phonetic Conference (4) we render the syllabic and non-syllabic function of a phoneme by the subscripts $_{\circ}$ and $_{\wedge}$ respectively, voicing by $_{\mathbf{,}}$ and voicelessness by $_{\mathbf{v}}$.

The examples quoted within diagonals present the phonemic ("broad") transcription which analyzes speech into phonemes. The examples quoted in square brackets give the phonetic ("narrow") transcription which is concerned with the variety of speech sounds emitted, without reference to their function in language. Examples given in conventional spelling form are underlined.

Many problems which are merely mentioned in passing will be discussed by us elsewhere. A more detailed treatment of the theoretical questions outlined in Chapter I and particularly of the relation between the sound shape and its functions in language will be given in a future publication (5), where also our analysis of the English phonemic pattern will be discussed more explicitly.

The mathematical treatment of the information carried by the distinctive features within a message and of their information capacity within a given language code is the subject of a special study being prepared in collaboration with Professor W. Hurewicz of the Department of Mathematics of M.I.T.

We are greatly indebted to Professor L. L. Beranek, Technical Director of the Acoustics Laboratory, M.I.T., and to Professor S. S. Stevens, Director of the Psychological Laboratories, Harvard University, for the many valuable suggestions which they made upon reading our manuscript. We are grateful to Dr. G. von Békésy, Senior Research Fellow in Psychophysics at Harvard University, for his illuminating comments on many of the problems involved. The inspired participation of Professor John Lotz in various stages of our discussions greatly contributed to their progress. We thank Professors W. Hurewicz, J. C. R. Licklider, and W. A. Rosenblith, M.I.T., for their stimulating remarks.

This publication could hardly have been completed without the help of Professor W. N. Locke, Head of the Department of Modern Languages, M.I.T., who contributed generously both time and advice.

We wish to acknowledge further the contributions of Mr. R. F. Schreitmueller, Dr. K. N. Stevens and other members of the staffs of the Acoustics Laboratory and the Research Laboratory of Electronics, M.I.T., where a large part of this research has been carried on in connection with projects financed under grants from the U. S. Air Force and the Carnegie Foundation.

The research project in modern Russian at the Department of Slavic Languages and Literatures, Harvard University, generously supported by the Rockefeller Foundation, and especially the superb x-ray studies made as part of this research by Dr. A. S. MacMillan and Dr. George Kelemen at the Massachusetts Eye and Ear Infirmary, Harvard Medical School, clarified many crucial points.

For our spectrograms we used records kindly provided by Professor Marguerite Durand, Institut de Phonétique, Paris, for French; by Dr. F. S. Cooper, Associate Research Director of Haskins Laboratories, Professor John Lotz and Dr. A. Kuypers for Circassian; by Professor Clyde Kluckhohn, Harvard University, for Navaho; by Professor E. Westphal of the London School of Oriental and African Studies for Xhosa. Professor Osman Kemal Mawardi, M.I.T., Dr. Hari Keshab Sen, Harvard College Observatory, and Mr. Esat Turak, Harvard School of Design, graciously consented to serve as native speakers for spectrograms of Arabic, Bengali and Turkish. We owe thanks also to Mr. L. G. Jones of Northeastern University for spectrograms of English and for kindly communicating to us the results of his own experiments.

We want to express our particular gratitude to Avis M. Tetley, who has been both patient and efficient in seeing the manuscript through the press.

Criticisms and comments on any of the facts, concepts, terms, or interpretations presented in this report will be appreciated.


Cambridge, December 1951

Since the first edition of our Preliminaries is out of print and the demand for copies continues, we are publishing this second printing. The corrections and additions were made possible through the numerous valuable suggestions received from our correspondents. We are especially indebted to Professors C. H. Borgström (University of Oslo), K. Bouda (University of Erlangen), T. M. Camara (Rio de Janeiro), E. Fischer-Jørgensen (University of Copenhagen), R-M. S. Heffner (University of Wisconsin), W. Z. Leopold (Northwestern University), C. Lévi-Strauss (University of Paris), H. Penzl (University of Michigan), K. L. Pike (University of Michigan), T. H. Sebeok (Indiana University), K. Togeby (University of Copenhagen), W. F. Twaddell (Brown University) and H. Werner (Clark University). Mr. G. de Saussure

(M.I.T.) kindly served as native speaker for our new French spectrograms and enabled us to confirm the phonemic definition of nasality proposed in the Cours de Linguistique of his grandfather.  The Electronics Research Project of Northeastern University graciously permitted us to reproduce the instructive intervalgrams of the English stops executed there by Mr. Jacob Wiren. We thank Mr. E. D. Canonge, Summer Institute of Linguistics, Norman, Oklahoma, for the Comanche records and their phonemic transcription.

Cambridge, May 1952

The present reissue, which reproduces unchanged the text of the second printing, has been made necessary by the continuing demand for <u>Preliminaries to Speech Analysis.</u>  We had hoped to publish a revised edition of the monograph at this time, but work on the revision has taken longer than originally expected.  Some of the material that will be included in the revised edition may be found in the following articles and books:

1.  Roman Jakobson and Morris Halle:  <u>Fundamentals of Language</u>  (The Hague, 1956); Germ. trans. by G. F. Meier <u>Grundlagen der Sprache</u> (Berlin, 1960)

2.  Roman Jakobson and Morris Halle: "Phonology in Relation to Phonetics," in L. Kaiser ed., <u>Manual of Phonetics,</u> (Amsterdam, 1957) pp. 215–251

3.  Morris Halle: "In Defence of the Number Two," <u>Studies Presented to J. Whatmough</u> (The Hague, 1957) pp. 65–72

4.  Roman Jakobson:  "Mufaxxama: The Emphatic Phonemes of Arabic," <u>Studies Presented to J. Whatmough</u> (The Hague, 1957) pp. 105–115

5.  Morris Halle: "Questions of Linguistics," <u>Il Nuovo Cimento,</u> Suppl. to vol. 13, series X, pp. 494–517 (1959)

6.  Morris Halle: <u>The Sound Pattern of Russian</u> (The Hague, 1959)

7.  Gunnar Fant: <u>Acoustic Theory of Speech Production</u> (The Hague, 1960)

8.  Roman Jakobson and Morris Halle: "Tenseness and Laxness"

Roman Jakobson, Harvard University
C. Gunnar M. Fant, Royal Institute of Technology, Stockholm
Morris Halle, Massachusetts Institute of Technology

Cambridge, September 1961

The text of the present printing remains unchanged except for the addition of the article "Tenseness and Laxness" on page 57.

Cambridge, August, 1963

# I  THE CONCEPT OF THE DISTINCTIVE FEATURE

## 1.1  RESOLVING SPEECH INTO ULTIMATE UNITS.

In a typical test of the intelligibility of speech, an English speaking announcer pronounces isolated root words (bill, put, fig, etc.), and an English speaking listener endeavors to recognize them correctly. For the listener this situation is in one sense simpler than normal speech communication because the word samples with which he deals cannot be broken up into shorter meaningful entities and are not grouped into higher units.  Thus the division of sentences into words and of words into their grammatical components does not concern this listener.  Nor need he account for the interrelation of words within a sentence and of various grammatical components within a complex word (ex-port-s, im-port-ed, re-port-ing, mid-night).

In another sense, however, this test is more complicated than normal speech communication.  Neither the context nor the situation aids the listener in the task of discrimination.  If the word bill were to appear in the sequence one dollar bill or as a single word said to a waiter after a meal, the listener would be able to predict its appearance.  In such a situation, the sounds which compose this word are redundant to a high degree, since they "could have been inferred a priori"(1). If, however, the word is deprived of any prompting context, either verbal or non-verbal, it can be recognized by the listener only through its sound-shape.  Consequently, in this situation the speech sounds convey the maximum amount of information.

The question arises:  how many significant units, i.e., units relevant for the discrimination of the samples, do the sound-shapes of the samples contain? Upon perceiving syllables such as bill and pull, the listener recognizes them as two different words distinguishable by their initial part /bi/ and /pu/ respectively.  This distinctive fraction, however, may be decomposed in turn. The listener, and any member of the English speech community, has in his vocabulary words such as pill and bull.  On the one hand, identical means are employed for distinguishing bill from pill and bull from pull.  On the other hand, the distinction between bill and bull is the same as that between pill and pull. Thus to distinguish between bill and pull a double operation is necessary.  The fraction /bi/ in bill proves capable of being split into two segments /b/ and /i/, the first exemplified by the pair bill - pill and the second by bill - bull.

Each of the two segments derived serves to distinguish the word bill from a whole series of vocables, all other things being equal.*  For each of them a set of other segments can be substituted.  This substitution of one segment by others is called commutation.

---

* Henceforth we shall use the more condensed Latin equivalent of this formula: ceteris paribus.

We can list one whole commutation set. Commuting the first segment we obtain the series bill - pill - vill - fill - mill - dill - till - thill - sill - nil - gill /gil/ - kill - gill /ʒil/ - chill - hill - ill - rill - will. A closer examination of such a series permits certain inferences.

For some pairs of words in this set the discriminatory minimum is identical; hence one is warranted in saying that bill is to pill, as vill is to fill, or dill to till, or gill to kill, etc. or, for the sake of a more graphic presentation: bill:pill ≃ vill:fill ≃ dill:till ≃ gill:kill etc.

By the same token,
1) bill : vill ≃ pill : fill ≃ till : sill etc.
2) bill : mill ≃ dill : nil etc.
3) bill : dill ≃ pill : till ≃ fill : sill ≃ mill : nil etc.

A distinction is called minimal if it cannot be resolved into further distinctions which are used to differentiate words in a given language. We owe this term to Daniel Jones, from whom we also borrow the following definition*: "Wider differences may be termed duple, triple, etc., according to the number of minimal distinctions of which the total difference is composed. Duple distinctions are the result of two minimal distinctions." (2)

The distinctions between bill and pill, or bill and vill or bill and dill are minimal distinctions since they cannot be resolved into simpler discriminations, which are, in turn, capable of differentiating English words. On the other hand, the relation of bill to till is a duple distinction, composed of two minimal distinctions: 1) bill - dill (which is equivalent to the distinction pill - till) and 2) bill - pill (equivalent of dill - till). The relation of bill to sill is a triple distinction: in addition to the two minimal distinctions cited, it includes a third one: bill - vill (equivalent to pill - fill and to till - sill).

The discrimination between the words bill and fell implies a duple distinction in their initial segments (/b/ - /f/), and a minimal one in the middle segments (/i/ - /e/). To discriminate between words such as bit and said, we need a triple distinction in their first segment and one minimal distinction in each of the two others.

Without further examples, it becomes clear that the listener of a speech sample is faced with a series of two-choice selections. To identify the message bill, he must decide for the non-vocalic inception against the vocalic and for the consonantal against the non-consonantal. By this double operation, vowels, liquids and glides are eliminated because if the word had begun with a vowel,

* We, alone, are responsible for the way in which these concepts are hereafter applied to the empirical material.

the inception would have been identified as vocalic and non-consonantal; if with a liquid, as both vocalic and consonantal; and if with a glide, as neither vocalic nor consonantal. (For the interpretation of these distinctions see Sec. 2.2).

The next decision to be made is between bill and gill /gil/ - diffuse or compact (see 2.41), between bill and dill - grave or acute (see 2.42), and finally, between bill and mill - non-nasalized or nasalized (see 2.44). A decision in favor of the latter of the two alternatives would leave no further selections, since /m/ is the only combination of grave and nasal in English. But the opposite choice being made, there inevitably follows the selection between bill and pill - weak or strong (in more general terms, lax or tense: see 2.43), and, finally, the selection between bill and vill - stop or constrictive (in more general terms, interrupted or continuant: see 2.311). An analogous sequence of operations treats the two succeeding segments of the sample /i/ and /l/. The set of selections to be made is, however, more restricted than for the initial segment. For example, when a sequence begins with a stop, as bill does, the option for vocalic is obligatory, since in English the initial stop may be followed only by vowels or liquids.

Any minimal distinction carried by the message confronts the listener with a two-choice situation. Within a given language each of these oppositions has a specific property which differentiates it from all the others. The listener is obliged to choose either between two polar qualities of the same category, such as grave vs. acute, compact vs. diffuse, or between the presence and absence of a certain quality, such as voiced vs. unvoiced, nasalized vs. non-nasalized, sharpened vs. non-sharpened (plain). The choice between the two opposites may be termed distinctive feature. The distinctive features are the ultimate distinctive entities of language since no one of them can be broken down into smaller linguistic units. The distinctive features combined into one simultaneous or, as Twaddell aptly suggests, concurrent bundle form a phoneme.

For example, the word bill is comprised of three consecutive bundles of distinctive features: the phonemes /b/, /i/ and /l/. The first segment of the word bill is the phoneme /b/ consisting of the following features: 1) non-vocalic, 2) consonantal, 3) diffuse, 4) grave, 5) non-nasalized (oral), 6) lax, 7) interrupted. Since in English 7) implies both 1) and 2), the latter two features are redundant. Similarly 3) is redundant as it is implied by 4).

A speech message carries information in two dimensions. On the one hand, distinctive features are superposed upon each other, i.e., act concurrently (lumped into phonemes), and, on the other, they succeed each other in a time series. Of these two arrangements the superposition is the primary because it can function without the sequence; the sequence is the secondary since it implies the primary. For example, the French words où /u/ "where", eu /y/ "had" (participle), y /i/ "there", eau /o/ "water", oeufs /ø/ "eggs", et /e/ "and", aie /e/ "have!", un /ø̃/ "one", an /ã/ "year", etc., each contains a single phoneme.

The difference between the distinctive features of contiguous bundles permits the division of a sequence into phonemes. This difference may be either complete, as between the last two phonemes /i/ and /p/ in the word wing (which have no distinctive features in common) or partial, as between the last two phonemes of the word apt - /p/ and /t/ all of whose distinctive features are the same except one: /p/ is grave and /t/ is acute.

This suprasegmental extension of certain features such as interruptedness, diffuseness or non-nasality is selective: cf. such sequences as asp (continuant and interrupted), act (compact and diffuse) and ant (nasal and oral). On the other hand, strong (tense) and weak (lax) consonants cannot follow each other within a simple English word: cf. nabs/nabz/, nabbed/nabd/, and naps /naps/, napped/napt/. That is to say, in consonant sequences the tenseness and laxness features are suprasegmental.

Any one language code has a finite set of distinctive features and a finite set of rules for grouping them into phonemes and also for grouping the latter into sequences; this multiple set is termed phonemic pattern.

Any bundle of features (phoneme) used in a speech message at a given place in a given sequence is a selection from among a set of commutable bundles. Thus by commuting one feature in the first phoneme of the sequence pat we obtain a series bat - fat - mat - tat - cat. Any given sequence of phonemes is a selection from among a set of permutable sequences: e.g. pat - apt - tap. However, /tp'a/ not only does not, but could not exist as an English word, for it has an initial stop sequence and a single final vowel under stress, both of which are inadmissible according to the coding rules of contemporary English.

## 1.2 INVARIANCE AND REDUNDANT VARIATIONS

The consonants are quite different in the English coo and key or in the French coup and qui. In both languages a more backward (velar) articulation is used before /u/ and a more forward (palatal) articulation before /i/. The formants of the consonant are closely adapted to those of the following vowels, so that the frequency spectrum of /k/ before /u/ has a lower center of area and is closer to that of /p/ than is the case before /i/, where it has a higher center of area and is closer to that of /t/. Both in English and French, /p/ and /t/ are separate phonemes opposed to each other as grave and acute, whereas the two varieties of /k/ represent but a single phoneme. This seeming discrepancy is due to the fact that the opposition of /p/ and /t/ is autonomous, i.e. both /p/ and /t/ occur in identical contexts (pool - tool; pea - tea), while the difference between the two k-sounds is induced by the following vowel: it is a contextual variation. The retracted articulation and the low frequencies of one of these k-sounds and the more advanced articulation and high frequencies of the other are not distinctive but redundant features, since the distinction is carried by the subsequent vowels. In Roumanian, both k-sounds in question occur in one and the same context (e.g. before /u/: cu "with", with a backward articulation, and chiu "cry", with a more forward articulation) and, therefore, they represent two different phonemes.

In the same way, the difference between the so-called "clear" and "dark" varieties of the English /l/ is redundant: the "clear" variant indicates that a vowel follows and the "dark" variant that no vowel follows; thus in lull, the initial /l/ is "clear" and the final, "dark". In Polish these two sounds may appear in one and the same context and form a distinctive opposition: cf. the "clear" /l/ in laska "cane" and the sound close to the English "dark" variety in łaska "grace."

The relation between tart and dart, try and dry, and bet and bed represents in English one and the same minimal distinction regardless of the perceptible articulatory and acoustical difference between the three t-sounds cited. The invariant is the opposition of strength and weakness (for more precise data see 2.43). In English a regular concomitant factor of this opposition is the voicelessness of the strong consonants and the voicing of the weak ones. But this redundant feature may disappear occasionally; cf. the voiceless variants of /b d z/ observed by English phoneticians.

It is important to note that gradations in strength serve no distinctive purpose: they depend entirely upon the context. For instance, the heavy aspiration of the initial strong /p t k/ before a stressed vowel as in tart and, conversely, the lack of aspiration before other phonemes as in try are only contextual variants which cannot impede the identification of any /p t k/ as strong in contradistinction to the weak /b d g/.

Danish is another language that exhibits the opposition of strong and weak consonants. This opposition is implemented in different ways depending upon the position of the consonant in a word. Two positions are discernible in the Danish word - strong and weak. In monosyllabic words the strong position for a consonant is at the beginning of the syllable and the weak position, at its end. In strong position the strong stops are normally produced with a heavy aspiration, while their weak opposites appear as weak stops (differing from the English /b d g/ through voicelessness); e.g. tag "roof" - dag "day". In weak position the strong /t/ is weakened to the level of /d/, while its weak opposite is further weakened from /d/ to the weakest level /ð/ resembling somewhat the consonant of the English the; for example: hat [had] "hat" - had [haö] "hate". Consequently, the opposition of the strong and weak phoneme remains invariant in both positions; at the same time there is a redundant shift of both opposites induced by the weak position, which indicates that neither a stressed nor a long vowel follows. Although the weak phoneme in strong position and the strong phoneme in weak position overlap phonetically, in the strictly relational terms of distinctive features there is no overlapping:

"Two patterns are identical if their relational structure can be put into a one-to-one correspondence, so that to each term of the one there corresponds a term of the other" (3).

Hence, an automatic detector designed to distinguish between the two positions and between the two polar terms within each of them would unerringly "recognize" both the strong and weak phoneme:

|           | Position |      |
|-----------|----------|------|
| Phoneme   | Strong   | Weak |
| strong /t/ | t       |      |
| weak /d/  | d        | d    |
|           |          | ð    |

The instances cited show how the invariance of the minimal distinctions can be separated from the redundant features that are conditioned by the adjacent phonemes in the sequence.

The sequential arrangement of distinctive features does not generate the only type of redundancies. Another less analyzed though very important class of redundancies is conditioned by the superposition of simultaneous distinctive features. There are languages in which the velar [k] is in complementary distribution with the corresponding palatal stop or with a still more advanced prepalatal affricate (pronounced as in the English chew). For instance, the velar sound occurs only before back vowels and the palatal (or prepalatal) sound only before the front vowels. In such cases the former and the latter are considered two contextual variants representing a single phoneme. By the same reasoning, if in French we find the velar stop /k/, the palatal nasal /ɲ/ (as in ligne) and the prepalatal constrictive /ʃ/ (as in chauffeur), we must consider the difference between this velar, palatal and prepalatal articulation as entirely redundant, for this difference is supplementary to other, autonomous distinctions. All of these consonants are opposed to those produced in the front part of the mouth as compact vs. diffuse (see 2.41). When the features of interruptedness (stop), nasalization and continuancy are superposed upon the compactness feature, they are accompanied, in the French consonants, by the redundant features of velarity, palatality, and prepalatality respectively. Thus the French /p b/ and /t d/ bear the same relation to /k g/, as /f v/ and /s z/ do to /ʃ ʒ/, and as /m/ and /n/ to /ɲ/.

The redundant character of the velar and prepalatal feature of the English compact consonants can be demonstrated in a similar manner. In Czech or Slovak, however, the analogous difference between velars and palatals (including the prepalatals in the latter class) is distinctive, since these languages have velars and palatals, ceteris paribus. The velar stop /k/ is opposed to the palatal stop /c/ and the velar constrictive /x/ to the (pre)palatal /ʃ/. Consequently, in these languages the opposition grave vs. acute characterizes not only the relation of labials to dentals but also that of velars to palatals: /k/ is to /c/ as /p/ is to /t/.

The multiplicity of distinctions traditionally accepted in the analysis of speech could be radically diminished were we to eliminate the redundancies linked to the relevant opposition of vowels and consonants. For example, it can be shown that the relation of the close to the open vowels, on the one hand, and that of the labials and dental consonants to consonants produced against the hard or soft palate, on the other, are all implementations of a single opposition: diffuse vs. compact (see 2.41); provided that the numerous redundancies contingent upon the fundamental difference between the vocalic and consonantal feature be eliminated. In their turn the relations between the back and front vowels, and between the labial and dental consonants pertain to a common opposition grave vs. acute (see 2.421).

While the relational structure of these features, which are common to consonants and vowels, manifests a definite isomorphism (one-to-one correspondence), the variations are in complementary distribution. That is to say, they are determined by the different contexts in which they appear: the variations are dependent upon whether the gravity-acuteness and compactness-diffuseness features are superposed upon a vowel or a consonant.

By successively eliminating all redundant data (which do not convey new information) the analysis of language into distinctive features overcomes the "non-uniqueness of phonemic solutions" (4). This pluralism, pointed out by Y. R. Chao, interfered with the analysis as long as the phoneme remained the ultimate operational unit and was not broken down into its constituents. The present approach establishes a criterion of the simplicity of a given solution, for when two solutions differ, one of them is usually less concise than the other by retaining more redundancy.

The principle of complementary distribution, which has proven most efficacious in speech analysis, opens many new possibilities when its ultimate logical implications are made explicit. Thus if certain phonemic distinctions possess a common denominator and are never observed to co-exist within one language, then they may be interpreted as mere variants of a single opposition. Furthermore, the question can be raised whether the selection of a given variant in a certain language is not connected with some other features proper to the same linguistic pattern.

In this way the inquiry succeeds in reducing the list of distinctive features ascertained in the languages of the world. Trubetzkoy (5) distinguishes the following three consonantal oppositions: first, the opposition of strong and weak consonants, the former characterized by a stronger resistance to the air flow and stronger pressure; second, the opposition of a stronger and weaker resistance alone, without accompanying pressure differences; third, the opposition of aspirated and non-aspirated. Since, however, never more than one of these three oppositions has been encountered functioning autonomously within any one language, all three should be regarded as mere variants of a single opposition. Moreover, this variation is apparently redundant because it depends upon certain other consonantal features present in the same pattern (see 2.43).

The extremely limited set of distinctive features underlying a language, the restrictions on their actual combinations into bundles and sequences and, finally, a high amount of redundancy, lighten the load imposed upon the participants of the speech event.

In the hierarchy of the sound features the distinctive features are of paramount importance. However, the role of the redundancies must not be underestimated. Circumstances may even cause them to substitute for the distinctive features. In Russian the distinction between the palatalized and non-palatalized consonants plays a significant part in differentiating words. Palatalization produces a slight rise of the formants (see 2.423). The phoneme /i/ is implemented as a back vowel [ɨ] after non-palatalized consonants, and as a front vowel [i] in all other positions. These variants are redundant, and normally for Russian listeners it is the difference between the non-palatalized [s] and the palatalized [s̨] which serves as the means of discriminating between the syllables [sɨ] and [s̨i]. But when a mason telephoned an engineer saying that the walls [sɨrʲˈejut] "are getting damp" and the transmission distorted the high frequencies of the [s] so that it was difficult to comprehend whether the walls "were getting damp" or "turning gray" [s̨irʲˈejut], then the worker repeated the word with particular emphasis on the [ɨ] , and through this redundant feature the listener made the right choice. In S. S. Stevens' formulation:

> "…..the fact of redundancy increases the reliability of speech communication and makes it resistant to many types of dis- ² tortion. By limiting the number of discriminations required of the listener and by assisting his choice through the redundant coding of information, we make talking to one another a reasonably satisfactory business" (6).

## 1.3 IDENTIFICATION OF DISTINCTIVE FEATURES

Any distinctive feature is normally recognized by the receiver if it belongs to the code common to him and to the sender, is accurately transmitted and has reached the receiver.

Suppose that both participants of the speech event use the same kind of standard English and that the listener has received the vocables gip, gib and gid, which are unfamiliar to him, as to many other English speakers. He does not know that gip means "to clean (fish)", gib, "castrated tom-cat", and gid, "an animal disease." Yet the information he obtains from these three samples is that they may be English words, since none of the features and feature combinations contained in them contradict the English code. Moreover, the three samples convey the information that, if they are words, then each of them has a different meaning, for there is a duple distinction between gip and gid and two different minimal distinctions separate gib from gip and gid. Were the English-speaking listener to hear the following highly improbable sentence: "The gib with the gid shall not gip it", he would know from his knowledge of the rules of the English code, that /gib/ ≠ /gip/ ≠ /gid/. Were the samples to be transmitted in a German speech circuit, <u>gib</u> and <u>gip</u> would be identified as two optional variants of what is probably the same word, since in German the distinction of /b/ and /p/ is cancelled at the end of the word. The same identification would be made in a Finnish speech circuit, since in the Finnish code the difference between the sounds [b] and [p] has no distinctive value.

Information Theory uses a sequence of binary selections as the most reasonable basis for the analysis of the various communication processes (7). It is an operational device imposed by the investigator upon the subject matter for pragmatic reasons. In the special case of speech, however, such a set of binary selections is inherent in the communication process itself as a constraint imposed by the code on the participants in the speech event, who could be spoken of as the <u>encoder</u> and the <u>decoder</u>.

This follows from the fact that the sole information carried by the distinctive feature is its distinctiveness. The listener distinguishes the word /gib/ from /gid/ by one feature: the grave character of /b/ as opposed, <u>ceteris paribus</u>, to the acute character of /d/. The same word /gib/ is distinguished from /gip/ by a different feature: the weak character of /b/ as opposed to the strong character of /p/. In these two examples, pairs of words display one minimal distinction in corresponding segments, <u>ceteris paribus.</u> Other pairs of words can display a higher number of minimal distinctions either in one segment or in more than one segment. When we review these minimal distinctions used to discriminate between these pairs of words, we find only two possibilities: a) occurrences of the same opposition (<u>gib:gid</u> ∼ <u>fat:sat</u>), and b) each of the two distinctions has a specific property of its own (<u>gib:gid</u> ≠ <u>gib:gip</u>).

To be sure, articulatorily, physically, and perceptually, there exists a continuous range of degrees from whisper to full voicing, but only two polar points - the presence and the absence of voice - are picked out as distinctive features. There is a continuous variation in the shape of the lips from a close rounding to spreading and in the corresponding acoustic effects; but the linguistic opposition flat vs. plain (e.g. German <u>Küste</u> "shore" - <u>Kiste</u> "box") is a linguistic assignment of distinctive value to two distant lip positions and to their contrastive acoustical effects (see 2.422). In general, no language possesses more than one minimal distinction based on the size of the lip orifice.

The dichotomous scale is the pivotal principle of the linguistic structure. The code imposes it upon the sound.

Only one phonemic relation presents a somewhat different aspect. This is the relation between vowels with a compact and those with a diffuse spectrum (open and close, in articulatory terms). In a language such as Turkish, the vowels are grouped into compact and diffuse pairs, other things being equal: /kes/ "cut!" is to /kis/ "tumor" as /kol/ "arm" is to /kul/ "slave". But a language such as Hungarian distinguishes, <u>ceteris paribus</u>, three degrees of compactness. Cf. /tår/ "bald" with an open rounded back vowel - /tor/ "feast" with the corresponding mid vowel - /tur/ "rakes up" with the close vowel, and, similarly, in the unrounded front series, /næ/ "take it!" - /ne/ "don't!" -

/ni/ "look!"*. The minimal distinction remains the same as in Turkish: /o/ and /e/ are opposed to /u/ and /i/ as <u>relatively</u> compact to <u>relatively</u> diffuse. In Hungarian, however, the same opposition (relatively compact vs. relatively diffuse) reappears in such pairs as /tår/ - /tor/ and /næ/ - /ne/; that is to say that /a/ : /o/∝/o/ : /u/. In this "phonemic proportion" /o/ (or /e/) functions as the "mean proportional." It carries two opposite features - compactness vs. the diffuse /u/ (or /i/) and diffuseness vs. the compact /a/ (or /æ/). (On ways of dealing with such bi-polar phonemes in analytical procedures see 2.414).

No other inherent phonemic oppositions exhibit such bi-polar complexes. There are, however, conjugate distinctions prone to merge, e.g., the pairs continuant - interrupted, and strident - mellow. When two conjugate oppositions merge the resulting opposition is maximally clearcut, optimal. Thus the optimal continuant consonants are strident; the optimal interrupted, mellow. A similar relation links the oppositions grave vs. acute and flat vs. plain. The optimal grave vowels are flat; the optimal acute are plain (concerning the reverse combinations of such features as interrupted strident, continuant mellow, flat acute or plain grave and ways of treating them in the analytical procedures see 2.324 and 2.4236).

It is the dichotomous scale of the distinctive features, in particular, and the whole patterning of the linguistic code, in general, that to a large extent determines our perception of the speech sounds. We perceive them not as mere sounds but specifically as speech components. More than this, the way we perceive them is determined by the phonemic pattern most familiar to us. Therefore, a monolingual Slovak identifies the rounded front vowel /φ/ of the French word <u>jeu</u> as /e/, since the only distinctive opposition in his mother tongue is acute (front) vs. grave (back) and not flat (rounded) vs. plain (unrounded). A monolingual Russian, on the contrary, perceives the same French vowel as /o/ because his native tongue possesses only the one of the two oppositions in question, namely, flat vs. plain. Even as expert a linguist as the Frenchman Meillet perceived the Russian sharpened /t/ as a sequence of /t/ and non-syllabic /i̯/ and not as a consonant with simultaneous, superposed sharpening (palatalization), for Meillet's judgment was based on his native French, which lacks the sharpening feature but possesses the non-syllabic /i̯/. Hence it is only to be expected that when nonsense syllables are used in intelligibility tests (traditionally called "articulation tests") the results depend upon whether or not these sequences are patterned in accordance with the rules of combination of the given linguistic code.

Interference by the language pattern affects even our responses to non-speech sounds. Knocks produced at even intervals, with every third louder, are per-

---

*The examples, which we have from John Lotz, belong to a colloquial variety of Standard Hungarian.

ceived as groups of three separated by a pause. The pause is usually claimed by a Czech to fall before the louder knock, by a Frenchman to fall after the louder; while a Pole hears the pause one knock after the louder. The different perceptions correspond exactly to the position of the word stress in the languages involved: in Czech the stress is on the initial syllable, in French, on the final and in Polish, on the penult. When the knocks are produced with equal loudness but with a longer interval after every third, the Czech attributes greater loudness to the first knock, the Pole, to the second, and the Frenchman, to the third.

If on the aural level too, speech analysis were to be conducted in terms of the binary phonemic oppositions, the task would be substantially facilitated and could perhaps supply the most instructive correlates of the distinctive features.

As to the acoustic investigation of the speech sounds, its whole development has been toward an ever more selective portrayal of the sound stimuli. Both the instruments used and the interpretation of the data recorded by them are progressively more oriented toward the extraction of the pertinent items. Investigators have come to see that the wave traces contain too much information and that means must be provided for selecting the essential information(8). As soon as it is realized that the proper criterion of selection is the linguistic relevance (expressed in binary terms), the acoustic problems of the speech sounds find a far more determinate solution. Correspondingly the articulatory stage of speech must be defined in terms of the means utilized to obtain any pair of contrastive effects. For example, as far as language uses an autonomous distinctive opposition of gravity and acuteness, we examine the acoustical correlates of the linguistic values in question and the articulatory prerequisites of these stimuli.

In short, for the study of speech sounds on any level whatsoever their linguistic function is decisive.

The interesting attempt, suggested by B. Bloch to decipher the phonemic pattern of a language from a mere examination of a sufficient number of recorded utterances (9) is onerous but feasible. It implies, however, two strictly linguistic assumptions. The first was formulated by Wiener (3): "In the problem of decoding, the most important information which we can possess is the knowledge that the message we are reading is not gibberish." This corresponds to the knowledge obtained by any listener upon reaching the so-called threshold of perceptibility, when the sounds heard begin to be perceived as speech sounds (10). Since it is speech, the second assumption follows as a corollary of the first: in its sound shape any language operates with discrete and polar distinctive features, and this polarity enables us to detect any feature functioning ceteris paribus.

Obviously such a task of deciphering becomes more difficult in the frequent cases called "switching code" by communication engineers (11) or "coexistent phonemic systems" by linguists (12). The Russian aristocracy of the last century with its bi-lingual speech - switching continually from Russian to French and vice versa even within a single sentence - provides a striking illustration. Another example is set by some Mohammedan cultural languages with their Arabic interpolations. Two styles of the same language may have divergent codes and be deliberately interlinked within one utterance or even one sentence. For instance, urban colloquial Czech is a whimsical oscillation between the literary language and vulgar Czech, each of them displaying its own phonemic pattern.

The dichotomous scale is superimposed by language upon the sound matter much in the same way as the diatonic scale is superimposed upon the sound matter by the musical pattern (13). But just as a musical scale cannot be grasped without reference to the sound matter, so in the analysis of the distinctive features such a reference is inevitable. Knut Togeby eloquently demonstrated this by a consistent assumption of the contrary (14). A distinctive feature cannot be identified without recourse to its specific property.

Such an investigation is supplemented but not supplanted by an inquiry into the distribution of these features in the speech sequences. M. Joos has observed, that since the diphthong /au/ (spelled ou as in council) is never followed within a simple English word by [p b f v m], this distributional feature defines the labial class of English consonants (15). Such a statement, however, presupposes the identification of each of the consonants in its various occurrences. We must know that /t/ in rout is identical with /t/ in rite which is opposed to /p/ in ripe as grave vs. acute, ceteris paribus. Otherwise, we would not know that in rout the diphthong /au/ is followed by /t/ and not by /p/, and we could not prove the above statement.

Thus for the identification of /p/, and of every other phoneme, a reference to the specific property of each of its distinctive features is imperative. But to which of the consecutive stages of the sound transmission shall we refer? In decoding the message received (A), the listener operates with the perceptual data (B) which are obtained from the ear responses (C) to the acoustical stimuli (D) produced by the articulatory organs of the speaker (E). The closer we are in our investigation to the destination of the message (i.e. its perception by the receiver), the more accurately can we gage the information conveyed by its sound shape. This determines the operational hierarchy of levels of decreasing pertinence: perceptual, aural, acoustical and articulatory (the latter carrying no direct information to the receiver). The systematic exploration of the first two of these levels belongs to the future and is an urgent duty.

Each of the consecutive stages, from articulation to perception, may be predicted from the preceding stage. Since with each subsequent stage the selectivity increases, this predictability is irreversible and some variables of any antecedent stage are irrelevant for the subsequent stage. The exact measurement of the vocal tract permits the calculation of the sound wave (16), but the same acoustical phenomenon may be obtained by altogether different means. Similarly, any given attribute of the auditory sensation may be the result of different physical variables (17) so that there is no one-to-one relation between the dimensions of the acoustical stimulus and the auditory attribute. The former cannot be predicted from the latter, but the totality of the dimensions of the stimulus renders the attribute predictable.

To sum up, the specification of the phonemic oppositions may be made in respect to any stage of the speech event from articulation to perception and decoding, on the sole condition that the variables of any antecedent stage be selected and correlated in terms of the subsequent stages, given the evident fact that we speak to be heard in order to be understood.

## 1.4 INHERENT AND PROSODIC DISTINCTIVE FEATURES

The distinctive features are divided into two classes: 1. inherent and 2. prosodic. The latter are superposed upon the former and are lumped together with them into phonemes. The opposition grave vs. acute, compact vs. diffuse, or voiced vs. unvoiced, and any other opposition of inherent distinctive features appears within a definite sequence of phonemes but is, nevertheless, definable without any reference to the sequence. No comparison of two points in a time series is involved. Prosodic features, on the other hand, can be defined only with reference to a time series. A few examples may clarify this statement.

A syllabic phoneme is opposed to the non-syllabic phonemes of the same syllable by a relative prominence. For the most part syllabicity is an exclusive function of the vowels. Cases when some vowels or liquids, ceteris paribus, carry the distinctive opposition syllabic vs. non-syllabic are particularly rare. For instance, the Old Czech sequence b r d u changes meaning depending upon the syllabic or non-syllabic character of the /r/ (see 2.226).

It is obvious that whether or not /r/ constitutes a maximum in loudness can only be determined by comparison with the loudness of the other phonemes of the same sequence.

In a sequence of syllables a relative prominence opposes one syllabic phoneme to the others of the same sequence as stressed vs. unstressed. In a number of languages words have, ceteris paribus, a different place of stress, for instance, English billow /b'ilou/ - below /bil'ou/. The greater and lesser prominence of syllabics is a relative notion which can be determined only by a comparison of all syllabics pertaining to the same sequence. The same holds when the distinctive role is played by the relation not of the loudness levels but of the pitch levels of the voice. In K. L. Pike's formulation, "the important feature is the relative height of a syllable in relation to the preceding or following syllables" (18).

When in place of or beside the level, the modulation plays a distinctive role, we identify the pitch or loudness contour of a phoneme by comparing two points in the time series. For instance, the Lithuanian falling pitch, which is opposed to the rising pitch and is due to a lowering of frequency, habitually accompanied by a decrease of amplitude, is identified by comparing the initial and final fractions of the vowel affected. By a similar comparison we identify the Danish "falling loudness of the voice" (the so-called stød), which is due to a decrease of amplitude often accompanied by a decrease of frequency (19).

The prosodic opposition long vs. short (distinguishing either simple from sustained or simple from reduced phonemes) is based on the relative, not absolute, length of the phonemes in the given sequence. Their absolute duration is a function of the speech tempo. For instance, in the Czech pravá práva/prava: pra:va/ "true rights", the first vowel of the first word is identified as short in relation to the second, long vowel, while the second word displays the inverse relation.

<h2 align="center">1.5 THE DISTINCTIVE FEATURES COMPARED TO<br>THE OTHER SOUND FEATURES</h2>

The smallest meaningful unit in language is called morpheme. A root, a prefix and a suffix are morphemes. A root word is a one morpheme word. The distinctive features and the phonemes possess no meaning of their own. Their only semantic load is to signalize that a morpheme which, ceteris paribus, exhibits an opposite feature is a different morpheme; cf. /gip/, /gib/ and /gid/. This discriminatory function may be assumed by more than one feature (and phoneme), as in the case of /bit/ and /sed/.

There is no difference in function between diverse features (and phonemes). For instance, the question of what is the specific denotation of nasal consonants or, in particular, of /m/ in English, makes no sense. /m/ in map, mess, aim has on the semantic level no common denominator which would set it off from /n/ or from /b/. This lack of semantic difference between diverse distinctive features makes them purely discriminatory marks which are otherwise empty. It separates them from all other sound features functioning in language. Only these, purely discriminatory and otherwise empty units are used to construct the whole stock of morphemes of all languages of the world.

Configurational features are features which signal the division of the sound chain of the utterance into grammatical units of different degrees of complexity. For instance, in languages where the stress is bound to the initial (or final) syllable and, consequently, cannot serve as a distinctive feature, it functions as a border mark which denotes the beginning (or end) of the word. On the contrary, in a language where the stress is free (i.e. can fall on any syllable in the word), its place performs a distinctive function and contains no specific denotation.

From the various redundant and expressive features of English intonation, Z. S. Harris (20) has extracted three configurational units: "/?/ for rise, /./ for fall, /,/ for middle register (as against low register) base-line". /./ denotes the end of the sentence, /,/ the end of a phrase in a sentence to be continued, and /?/ the question, which in configurational terms means the end of a sentence to be supplemented by an answer; i.e. the potential completeness of the utterance but incompleteness of the dialogue. When used as distinctive features, rise and fall have no other function than discrimination between morphemes, but when they serve as configurational features they carry a specific denotation; e.g. fall signifies the completeness of a sentence, and a rising intonation, even if superposed upon a mere nasal murmur, is immediately identified by English listeners as a question.

Expressive features are features which signal emotional attitudes of the speaker and the emphasis he puts on some of the particulars conveyed by his utterance. To use D. Jones' example (1), in the pronunciation of the English word enormous the emphasis may be effected "by an increase of strength coupled with an increase in the length of the vowel and the use of a special intonation" (a greater extent of the fall). In the expressive features, we deal with a special kind of relations. A neutral, unemotional variety is paired with the expressive variety which presents a "grading gamut" according to the term of Sapir, who defined this type of relation distinctly (21). Like the configurational features, the expressive features carry their specific denotation. In English the intensified stress, as opposed to the normal stress, denotes an emphatic attitude, and a further reinforcement of stress, a still more emphatic attitude.

The distinctive and the configurational features refer to the meaningful units of the utterance; the expressive features, to the speaker's attitude, and the redundant features (see 1.2) refer to other sound features: e.g. the redundant "clearness" of the English /l/ denotes that a vowel follows. Possession of a specific denotation unites the redundant features with the configurational and expressive features and separates them from the distinctive features. The "emptiness" of the distinctive features sets these apart from all other sound features.*

The following survey is confined to the inherent distinctive features. The prosodic features and other problems involving the sequential arrangement, in particular the segmentation of the sequence will be treated separately.

* In certain cases single distinctive features can assume an additional configurational function. In this function they obtain a positive denotation. For instance, in certain Scottish dialects where nasal vowels occur and are opposed to the oral vowels in the first syllable only (5), the occurence of a nasal vowel denotes the beginning of a word, but within the limits of the first syllable the opposition of nasal and oral vowels remains a "void" distinctive means.

# II A **TENTATIVE SURVEY OF** THE DISTINCTIVE FEATURES

## 2.1 PREFATORY ACOUSTICAL REMARKS

In the sound spectrograms* the frequency-intensity pattern of speech is portrayed as a function of time. In this "running frequency analysis" the statistical properties of the speech wave are sampled within time intervals that are short compared to the duration of a phoneme. The spectrograms and the supplementary "cross sections" of intensity vs. frequency provide a source of information that may be rather confusing unless an optimal set of parameters is used in the analysis. These parameters can best be discovered by an analysis of language into distinctive features.

The speech wave may be considered as the output of a linear network; i.e., the vocal tract coupled to one or more sources. The speech wave has no other properties than those of the sources and the network. This relation may be written

$$W = T \cdot S$$

**where W represents the speech wave, T the transfer function of the network, and S the source. Two simultaneous sources may be handled by superposition:**

$$W = T_1 S_1 + T_2 S_2$$

Speech analysis shows that only a very limited number of characteristics of the source and of the transfer functions are utilized in the various languages of the world for semantic discriminations. These characteristics are described in the following paragraphs.

### 2.11 Properties of the Source Function Utilized in Language

2.111 Type of Source. There are basically two kinds of sources, periodic and noise sources. A periodic source is manifested by a characteristic harmonic structure in the spectrogram. A noise source, on the other hand, causes an irregular distribution of energy in the time dimension. These two sources can be simultaneously active in the production of a single phoneme.

2.112 Number of Sources. Some sounds such as [v] or [z] have two sources. One of these is located at a point of maximum stricture in the vocal tract, while the other, i.e. the so-called voice, is located at the larynx and is more or less periodic. A source which lies above the larynx in the vocal tract produces anti-resonances in the transfer function (cf. 2.122).

---

* The sound spectrograms to which reference is made in this report either are of the type produced by the Kay Electric Company Sonagraph or are from the book Visible Speech by Potter, Kopp, and Green (1).

2.113 Transient Effects.    The manner in which the source is turned on and off is linguistically significant. We distinguish abrupt onsets and declines from smooth ones. For example, in the phoneme /ʃ̂/ as in chip we have an abrupt onset, while in /ʃ/ as in ship the onset is smooth.

## 2.12  Transfer Functions Utilized in Language

2.121 General Properties.    In the mathematical treatment of the transmission properties of the vocal tract it has been found convenient to utilize the techniques and concepts developed for network analysis (2).  One of the standard cases treated in network analysis is a lossless transmission line with no branches in parallel, where the input (source) is located at one end of the line and the output measured at the other.  The intensity vs. frequency spectrum of the output of such a transmission line can be completely specified by stating the frequencies at which the output will be infinite (resonance).  In network analysis it is usual to call these resonance frequencies poles.

When in a lossless line, some of these conditions are not fulfilled, e.g. the source is not located at the end of the line, then the output will deviate from that in the case discussed above:  in certain frequency regions there will be no output.  It is possible to view the deviation as due to an anti-resonance or zero which suppresses the energy in a given frequency region; i.e. acts like a resonance in reverse.  Thus, in order to specify the intensity vs. frequency spectrum of the output of any lossless system, it is sufficient to state the frequencies of the poles and the zeros (if any).

When a system contains small losses, the responses at resonance and anti-resonance are finite. In the complex frequency notation the poles and the zeros then have two parts, one giving the frequency location of the resonance or anti-resonance, and the other specifying the amount of damping (damping constant).

The poles depend primarily on the electrical properties of the series transmission line. In the case of speech this means that the poles depend upon the configuration of the vocal tract.  The zeros, on the other hand, depend primarily upon the interaction of parallel branches.  In speech that would mean that they depend upon the interaction of the two resonating systems in parallel which are created either by a) the opening of a supplementary passage or by b) the non-terminal location of the source.

When the location of a zero is close to that of a pole, the zero tends to cancel the effect of the pole. As the separation between them increases, the suppression decreases.

2.122 Location of Source.    In general the zeros occur at frequencies at which the impedance arising from the source in the direction opposite to the air flow is infinite.  A source located at the larynx will cause no anti-resonances of importance in the transfer function.  It is for this reason that we can specify vowels completely by the poles which give the frequency positions and bandwidths (damping constants) of the formants. A source located above the larynx in the vocal tract between cavities that have finite coupling to each other introduces zeros into the transfer function.

2.123 Shape of the Vocal Tract. The poles of the transfer function are primarily related to the geometrical configuration of the vocal tract and are independent of the source and its location. Calculations on the basis of x-ray data lead to substantial agreement between the poles and zeros of the predicted and measured spectra (3).

### 2.13 Neutral Position of the Vocal Tract

In the following, reference will be made to the neutral position of the vocal tract. This is the position of the vocal organs for producing a very open [æ] With respect to its acoustic results this articulatory position can best be approximated by a single tube closed at one end. As is well known, a tube of length L closed at one end resonates at frequencies where L is an odd multiple of one quarter wavelength. Since the average length of the vocal tract of males is about 17.5 cm, the resonances appear at approximately 500, 1500, 2500 cps. etc. The neutral position is of importance for predicting the effects on formant positions of variations in the over-all length of the vocal cavity of different individuals (3). It also serves as a reference point for the tenseness feature (cf. below 2.431).

### 2.14 Phoneme Boundaries

For practical purposes each phoneme can be represented by a quasi-stationary spectrum in which the transfer function is invariable with respect to time, except in the manner stated for transient effects (cf. 2.113). These transient effects, which are produced by rapid variations in the source function, may serve to delimit the individual phonemes in the chain. Rapid variations in the transfer function caused by swift changes in the position of the articulating organs also indicate the beginning or end (boundary) of a phoneme. Here, however, the minimum rate of change must be determined experimentally for each case. Rapid fluctuations in the over-all intensity of the speech wave provide an additional means for determining the location of a phoneme boundary.

### 2.2 FUNDAMENTAL SOURCE FEATURES

This class consists of two binary oppositions: vocalic vs. non-vocalic and consonantal vs. non-consonantal.

### 2.21 Vocalic vs. Non-Vocalic

Phonemes possessing the vocalic feature have a single periodic ("voice") source whose onset is not abrupt.

Usually, the first three vocalic formants for male voices are found below 3200 cps. The vocalic formants have small damping which expresses itself in the relatively narrow bandwidth of the formants. Because of the negative slope of the "voice" spectrum, the lower formants have greater intensity. But because of the ear's higher sensitivity to loudness in the region about 1-2 kc. it appears likely that in perception the effect of the declining spectrum tends to be equalized.

## 2.22 Consonantal vs. Non-Consonantal

Phonemes possessing the consonantal feature are acoustically characterized by the presence of zeros that affect the entire spectrum (cf. 2.441).

2.221 Vowels and Consonants.     Vowels are phonemes possessing the vocalic feature and having no consonantal feature. A limited number of combinations of positions of the first three formants are significant for the identification of vowels. Information on the intensity level (other things being equal, vowels louder than other speech sounds), duration, rise and decay time of the sound furnish supplementary identifying criteria for vowels.

Consonants are phonemes possessing the consonantal feature and having no vocalic feature. Certain features of consonants are perceived most readily by the influence they exert over the formants of adjacent vowels, but even in the absence of any adjacent vowel, all the features of a consonant are perfectly recognizable; cf. the last phoneme in the English words whisk - whist - whisp or in the Russian words /l'ift/ "elevator" - /fiɲ'iftʲ/ "enamel", /b'ukʃ/ "of letters" - /xar'ukʃ/ "standard" (see Fig. 10).

2.222 Liquids.     The so-called liquids, i.e. the laterals (l-sounds) and the various intermittent r-sounds, have the vocalic as well as the consonantal feature: like vowels, the liquids have only a harmonic source; like consonants, they show significant zeros in their spectrum envelope. The formant structure of the liquids is basically similar to that of vowels. The configuration of their first three formants, however, usually differs from that of any vowel. In the beginning of a liquid we observe a very sudden downward shift of most formants which is due to the increased length of the resonator system in comparison with that of adjacent vowels. The over-all intensity of the liquids is considerably lower than that of the vowels.

2.223 Glides. The so-called glides (30), like the English h and the "glottal catch", are distinguished from the vowels in that they have either a non-harmonic source as in the case of [h] or a transient onset of the source as in [ʔ]. They are distinct from the consonants in that they have no significant zeros in their spectra.

2.224 Production.     Vowels have no obstructive barrier along the median line of the mouth cavity, whereas consonants have a barrier sufficient to produce either complete occlusion or a turbulent noise source. Liquids are complex structures: they have a greater axial length-dimension in the direction of the air flow and they combine closure and aperture, either intermittently or by barring the median way and opening a lateral by-pass. Glides are produced by a stream of air passing through the glottis when it is narrowed or just after an abrupt opening following complete closure.

2.225 Perception. The vowels have far higher power than the consonants. As determined by Sacia and Beck, the average power for different English vowels is from 9 to 47 microwatts, while for consonants it ranges between 0.08 and 2.11 microwatts(4).

2.226 Occurrence. The distinction between vowels and consonants is universal. In America and Africa there are a few native languages without liquids. Many languages, e.g. Italian and Russian, have no glide phonemes.

The vowels figure predominantly as syllabics and, vice versa, the role of syllabics is assumed primarily by vowels. Most of the vocalic phonemes occur only as syllabics. A few others, being preponderantly syllabic, lose their syllabicity in some positions. For instance, English unstressed /i/ and /u/ become non-syllabic when adjacent to any other vowel (including the stressed /i/ and /u/); e.g. boy, day, geese, yes, yield (phonetically [j'i:ld] and phonemically /i'iild/), out, soul, shoe, well, wood (phonetically [w'ud] and phonemically /u'ud/) woo (phonetically [w'u:] and phonemically /u'uu/).

It is rare for non-syllabic vowels to be autonomous phonemes that may occur in the same positions as the corresponding syllabic phonemes; e.g. Russian /'uḷii̯/ "hive" - /'uḷii̯/ "hives".

Phonemes other than vowels occur for the most part only as non-syllabics. A few others (mostly liquids or nasal consonants), being preponderantly non-syllabic, acquire syllabicity in some positions. For instance, the Czech r and l become syllabic when preceded by a non-syllabic and not followed by a syllabic. Compare such dissyllables as škrtl [ʃkr̩tl̩] "scrapped", trval [tr̩val] "lasted" and monosyllables as rval [rval] "tore" and zlo [zlo] "evil". Syllabic liquids occasionally appear as autonomous phonemes capable of occurring in the same position as the corresponding non-syllabic phonemes; e.g. in Old Czech: dissyllabic brdu /br̩du/ "to the summit" - monosyllabic brdu /brdu/ "I stroll".

A set of rules, some of them universal, determine the pattern of the syllable. For instance, there is no known language where a syllable cannot begin with a consonant or terminate in a vowel, whereas there is a number of languages in which a syllable cannot begin with a vowel or terminate in a consonant. Thus, for a sequence of phonemes, the contrast of vocality and non-vocality is of primary importance, while the occurence of these opposites in one and the same position is much more restricted: cf. English wet /u'et/, yet /i'et/ with vet, set, net, etc., or he /h'ii/ with his /h'iz/, hit /h'it/ etc.).

## 2.3 SECONDARY CONSONANTAL SOURCE FEATURES

This class includes:

1) two types of features due to the primary source:  a) envelope features, and b) the stridency feature,
2) the voicing feature due to a supplementary source.

### 2.31  Envelope Features

By the temporal envelope of sound intensity we mean the speech power averaged over about 0.02 seconds as a function of time.  There are two basic types of envelope: smooth and rough.  Phonemes with smooth envelopes have gradual onsets and decays and no abrupt changes in their temporal course.  Phonemes with rough envelopes have abrupt variations of power in their temporal course.  The latter can be subdivided into two groups depending upon whether or not there is sound after the abrupt variation in power.

Phonemes with smooth onsets are called continuants.  They are opposed to interrupted (more exactly, discontinuous) phonemes, which have an abrupt onset.  According to their decays, phonemes are divided into checked (with abrupt decays) and unchecked (with gradual decays.)

### 2.311  Interrupted vs. Continuant

2.3111 Stimulus.    The abrupt onset distinguishes the interrupted consonants (stops) from the continuant consonants (constrictives).  The onset of constrictives is gradual.  The main characteristic of stops, on the contrary, is a sharp wave front preceded by a period of complete silence, for which, under certain conditions, a mere vibration of the vocal bands may be substituted.  The spectrograms show here a sharp vertical line preceded either by a period of silence or a "voice bar" (1).

In English the abrupt onset of /p/ as in pill or of /b/ in bill is opposed to the smooth onset of /f/ as in fill or /v/ in vill.  Similarly, /t/ as in till is opposed to /θ/ in thill and to /s/ in sill.

In the liquids it is not primarily the onset and decline that serve a distinctive purpose, but rather the interruption of the sound course.  The continuant l-sound is opposed to the interrupted r-sound.  There are two varieties of the latter: the flap with a single interruption and the trill with recurrent interruptions, which is much more common.  Measurements of Czech trills show normally from two to three taps in the sound; in final position this may be reduced to a single tap, while the initial trill in emphasis has 4 to 5 taps.  The rate of the taps is approximately 25 per second.   There are languages, e.g. Mongolian, which have a considerably more rolled /r/ with a higher number of interruptions.  Examples of the interruption feature in Czech liquids: /kora:l/ "coral" - /kola:r/ "Roman collar".

As for the so-called "continuant r", it is actually a non-syllabic vowel. For example, the English "Received Pronunciation," possesses a vowel phoneme, which is opposed as diffuse to /a/, as grave to /i/ and as unrounded (plain) to the rounded (flat) /u/. This phoneme is split on the prosodic level into an unstressed /ə/ and a stressed /'ə/. The former loses its syllabicity in the neighborhood of another vowel phoneme (bear /b'eə/) and becomes still "closer" when followed by a vowel (red /ɹ'ed/). The stressed phoneme /'ə/ is represented by a more advanced and close variant before an unstressed /ə/ (bird /b'əəd/) and by a more retracted and open variant [ʌ] in other positions (bud / b'əd/).

2.3112 Production.    The stops have complete closure followed by opening. The constrictives have incomplete closure; but the narrowing considerably reduces the contribution of the cavities behind the point of articulation (3). The continuant liquids, i.e. laterals like /l/, combine a median closure with a side opening, whereas in the interrupted liquids like /r/, complete or partial cut-off of the air stream is effected by one or more taps of the apex of the tongue, or of the uvula.

2.3113 Perception.    Experiments conducted by L. G. Jones at Northeastern University have demonstrated that when the onset of a constrictive like [s] or [f] is erased from a recording, the sound perceived is a stop: [š] or [t] for the [s]; [f] or [p] for the [f]. (On the distribution of these two alternative perceptions see Sec. 2.323).

2.3114 Occurrence.    The opposition of interrupted (stops) and continuant consonants (constrictives) is found in most languages. As a rule, the number of constrictives in a language is lower than that of the stops and occasionally the class of constrictives contains but a single phoneme, usually /s/. In languages in which the opposition of constrictives and stops is not autonomous, it is either a concomitant of the opposition strident vs. mellow (see below 2.324), or, all the consonants are stops in contradistinction to the vowels. The latter is the case in some languages of Oceania and Africa.

In a great number of languages, for example in nearly all languages of the Far East, liquids are not divided into interrupted and continuant phonemes. The liquid phoneme in these languages may be represented either by [l] as in Chinese, or by [r] as in Japanese, or by a complementary distribution of two contextual variants - [r] and [l] pertaining to one single liquid phoneme as in Korean. In Korean the liquid phoneme in prevocalic position is [r]; elsewhere it is [l]. For this reason the Korean alphabet has only one letter for the two sounds, in [maru] "floor" and [pal] "foot", for instance. By a Korean the Czech words /karar/, /volal/, /oral/ and /dolar/ are all perceived and reproduced as terminating in [-ral].

2.3115 Double Stops.    The peculiar consonants with a double closure, which are widespread in languages of South Africa, are but special forms of consonant clusters.  They are extreme cases of co-articulation, which is widely used in language for building up phonemic sequences (5).  In the production of such consonants, the two closures attain their release in immediate succession. Nevertheless, they are perceived as clusters since the two releases are not simultaneous despite the considerable contraction of the sequence, and since other types of clusters do not occur in these languages (or at least not in the same positions).  In the South African clicks that are produced by a sucking in of air, the more frontal closure, e.g. dental or palatal, is released first and then the velar, as can be seen in the spectrograms (Fig. 2).  The opposite order is shown in the African labio-velar stops spelled kp, gb.  Since they are produced by expiration, the velar closure is released before the labial (6).

### 2.312  Checked vs. Unchecked

2.3121 Stimulus.   An abrupt decay is the opposite of a smooth one.  In spectrograms, checked phonemes are marked by a sharper termination, but this is ordinarily less prominent than an abrupt onset.

2.3122 Production.   The air stream is checked by the compression or closure of the glottis.

2.3123 Occurrence.   Certain varieties of checked stops, called glottalized, are found in many native languages of America, Africa, the Far East and the Caucasus; e.g. the spectrograms of the Navaho and Circassian glotallized stops (for the latter see Fig. 1) disclose a striking similarity of structure.

Examples: checked vs. unchecked stops: Circassian /t'a/ "dig!" - /ta/ "we"; /c'a/ "name" - /ca/ "tooth"; /p'a/ "place" - /pa/ "be out of breath!".  Less clear and most uncommon is the glottalization of constrictives (7) observed in Tlingit (Northwestern America) and Kabardian (N. Caucasus).

In languages that have an opposition of checked and unchecked stops, the checked glide (called "glottal catch") is related to the unchecked (even or gradual) glide as a glottalized consonant is to the corresponding non-glottalized.

### 2.32  Strident vs. Mellow

2.321 Stimulus.   Sounds that have irregular waveforms are called strident. In the spectrogram such sounds are represented by a random distribution of black areas.  They are opposed to sounds with more regular waveforms.  The latter are called mellow and have spectrograms in which the black areas may form horizontal or vertical striations.  The proper measure for this property is an auto-correlation function.  Mellow sounds have a wider auto-correlation than the corresponding strident, ceteris paribus, i.e. if the sounds in question have been properly normalized.

In the case of constrictives, mellowness is a consequence of a limitation upon the randomness in the energy vs. frequency distribution.  While there are no clear formant regions observable in the spectrum of the strident /s/, we can easily discern them in the mellow /θ/ (see Fig. 3). The oscillograms show a distinctly higher periodicity and uniformity in mellow constrictives such as /θ/ in comparison with /s/ and other strident constrictives.

In the case of stops, mellowness is achieved by a limitation upon the randomness of the phase. Cf. the pertinent remark of Licklider:

> "..... the various frequency components of the white noise are assigned their phase angles at random; the frequency components of the single pulse all reach their maximum amplitudes at the time t = O, and they cancel one another at all other times. As a result, we hear the white noise as sshhhh and the single pulse as pt." (8)

Examples. Strident vs. mellow constrictives: English sin - thin /θ'in/, breeze /br'iiz/ - breathe /br'iið/; Ewe (West Africa) /fu/ "feather" - /ɸu/ "bone", /vu/ "tear" - /βu/ "boat"; Low Sorbian /ʃiɠ/ "to sew" - /çiʃ/ "calm", Circassian /χy/ "sea" - /xy/ "net". Strident and mellow stops: German Zahl, /ŝaːl/ "number" - Tal, /taːl/ "valley" - Pfanne, /p̂anə/ "pan" - Panne, /panə/ "breakdown", Czech čelo /ĵʃelo/ "brow" - telo, /celo/ "body"; Chuckchee (in Northeastern Siberia) /χ̂ale/ "cap" - /kale/ "drawing".

The strident stop is called affricate. The sequence of stop plus constrictive is distinguished from an affricate by an intervening intensity minimum, which can be observed on a display of the speech wave as a function of time. Cf. Polish czy /ĵʃi/ "or" - trzy /tʃi/ "three"; czech /ĵʃex/ "Czech" - trzech /tʃex/ "of three" (31).

2.322 Production. Strident phonemes are primarily characterized by a noise which is due to turbulence at the point of articulation. This strong turbulence, in its turn, is a consequence of a more complex impediment which distinguishes the strident from the corresponding mellow consonants: the labiodentals from the bilabials, the hissing and hushing sibilants from the non-sibilant dentals and palatals respectively, and the uvulars from the velars proper. A supplementary barrier that offers greater resistance to the air stream is necessary in the case of the stridents. Thus beside the lips, which constitute the sole impediment employed in the production of the bi-labials, the labiodentals involve also the teeth. In addition to the obstacles utilized in the corresponding mellow consonants, the sibilants employ the lower teeth (see Fig. 3) and the uvulars, the uvula. The rush of air against such a supplementary barrier following the release of the strident stops yields the characteristic fricative effect that distinguishes these from other stops.

2.323 Perception. Experiments of L. G. Jones in which the onset of recorded constrictives (like [s]) was erased showed that as long as the sound interval remained over 25 to 30 millisec., the consonant was identified by listeners as an affricate (like [ŝ]) while a shorter sound interval was identified as a mellow stop (like [t]).

2.324 Occurrence.    The maximum, hence optimal, distinction of consonants from vowels may be achieved either by the greatest muffling of sound or by the closest approximation to noise.  High degree of muffling is found in the mellow stops, while noise is best approximated by the strident constrictives. Thus the optimal constrictive is strident, while the optimal stop is mellow, and in numerous languages the opposition constrictive vs. stop merges with the opposition strident vs. mellow.  For instance, in French all constrictives are strident /f v s z ʃ ʒ / and all stops mellow /p b t d k g/.

In some of these languages the opposition strident vs. mellow alone is relevant and constant; the difference of constrictives and stops becomes a redundant feature which, under certain conditions, can fail to materialize.  This happens in Portuguese, where the intervocalic [d b g] become mellow constrictives [ð β ɣ] so that they are opposed to /z v ʒ / not by the stop feature but only by their mellowness.  In other languages with a fusion of both oppositions, the stridency feature may become redundant, if some of the stop phonemes, at least under certain conditions, are represented by affricates.

In addition to strident constrictives and mellow stops, many languages possess such classes of phonemes as strident stops (affricates) and/or mellow constrictives.  For example, German and Czech have beside /s/ and /t/ the corresponding affricate /ŝ/, cf. German reissen "to tear", reiten "to ride", reizen "to tease".  Moreover, beside /f/ and /p/ German includes /f̂/; and Czech has /f̂/ beside the strident constrictive /ʃ/ and the mellow stop /c/. On the other hand, beside /s z/ and /t d/ English possesses the mellow constrictives /θ ð/, both spelled th.

When, beside strident constrictives and mellow stops, a language possesses either corresponding strident stops as German or mellow constrictives as Arabic, this state may be interpreted in terms of one single opposition: optimal constrictive vs. optimal stop.  Should we symbolize the former by a "plus" and the latter, correspondingly, by a "minus", such a complex unit as a strident stop or mellow constrictive would be "±".  The same device is applicable also in the case when, as in English, one pair of optimal constrictive and optimal stop (e.g. /s/ - /t/) is supplemented by a mellow constrictive (/θ/) and another pair (/ʃ/ - /k/) by a strident stop (/f̂/): both of these complex units could be designated by the same symbol ±.  In the relatively few languages with all four members in one series, e.g. those North Caucasian languages which have the strident constrictive /χ/, the mellow stop /k/, the mellow constrictive /x/ and the strident stop /χ̂/, we must operate with two auto-, nomous oppositions - constrictive vs. stop and strident vs. mellow.  Furthermore, insofar as it is preferable to deal with simple two-choice situations and to exclude complexes, the two oppositions might be treated separately in the case of ternary series as well, e.g. in English.

In addition to consonants proper, liquids may participate in the opposition strident vs. mellow.  A few languages, e.g. Czech, have a strident counterpart of the phoneme /r/.  This sibilant variety of trill is spelled ř : cf. řada "row",

<u>rada</u> "council". Some American Indian, African and Caucasian languages contain strident counterparts of the /l/ phoneme - lateral affricates and/or constrictives (9). Despite the high damping of their formants all these phonemes retain manifest acoustic traces of their relation to liquids. They are liquids with superposed stridency (cf. below 2.441).

2.33 Supplementary Source: <u>Voiced vs. Voiceless</u>

2.331 Stimulus. The voiced or "buzz" phonemes as /d b z v/ vs. the voiceless or "hiss" phonemes are characterized by the superposition of a harmonic sound source upon the noise source of the latter (10). For the voiced consonants this means a joint presence of two sound sources. The spectrum of voiced consonants includes formants which are due to the harmonic source. The most striking manifestation of "voicing" is the appearance of a strong low component which is represented by the voice bar along the base line of the spectrogram (11).

2.332 Production. Voiced phonemes are emitted with concomitant periodic vibrations of the vocal bands and voiceless phonemes without such vibrations.

2.333 Occurrence. The use of the distinctive consonantal opposition voiced vs. voiceless is widespread in the world; e.g., in Europe it is found in all Slavic languages as well as in Hungarian: cf. Russian /don/ "Don" - /ton/ "tone". The extension of this feature to liquids is extremely rare; e.g. in Gaelic voiced /r l/ and the corresponding voiceless /r̬ l̬/ may occur in the same positions. (On the nasal consonants see 2.443).

Vowels are normally voiced. It is still questionable whether there are languages in which parallel to the consonantal opposition voiced vs. voiceless, there actually is a similar distinctive opposition of voiced and murmured vowels, as reported about a few American Indian languages, e.g., Comanche. Either the vocal murmur is not a distinctive feature and functions merely as a border mark, or it may be a concomitant of the tense-lax opposition (Fig. 12).

In languages lacking an autonomous opposition of voiced and voiceless consonants, the latter is either used as a mere concomitant of the opposition of lax and tense consonants, as in English (cf. 2.434), or oral consonants are normally voiceless, as in Finnish dialects. Here the difference between "hiss" and "buzz" acts as a concomitant factor of the consonant-vowel opposition. In some of these languages an automatic voicing of consonants takes place in certain phonemic contexts.

2.4 RESONANCE FEATURES

This class includes:
       1) three types of features generated in the basic resonator: a) the compactness feature, b) three tonality features, c) the tenseness feature,
       2) the nasalization feature due to a supplementary resonator.

## 2.41 Compact vs. Diffuse

2.411 Stimulus. Compact phonemes are characterized by the relative pre-dominance of one centrally located formant region (or formant). They are opposed to diffuse phonemes in which one or more non-central formants or formant regions predominate.

Compact vs. diffuse vowels: English (RP) pet /pʰet/ - pit /pʰit/; pat /pʰat/ - putt /pʰət/; pot /pʰot/ - put /pʰut/. Compact vs. diffuse consonants: kill - pill or till; shill - fill or sill; ding /dʰiŋ/ - dim or din. The Czech symmetric pat-tern of compact and diffuse oral consonants presents good examples of the one-to-one correspondence: ti /ci/ "they" - ty /ti/ "them"; šál /ʃaːl/ " shawl" - sál /saːl/ "hall; kluk /kluk/ "boy" - pluk /pluk/ "regiment"; roh /rox/ "horn" - rov /rof/ "grave".

In the case of the vowels this feature manifests itself primarily by the position of the first formant (11): when the latter is higher (i.e. closer to the third and higher formants), the phoneme is more compact. The closer the first formant is to the upper formants, the higher will be the intensity level of the region above the first formant, especially the level between peaks. (See Fig. 4.).

In the consonants, compactness is displayed by a predominant formant region, centrally located, as opposed to phonemes in which a non-central region pre-dominates; (cf. Fant's analysis of Swedish stops (3)).The compact nasals have a dominant formant region between the characteristic nasal formants (200 cps and 2500 cps). Delattre's observations on the positions of the first formant in stops and nasal consonants (12) corroborate the parallelism between the com-pactness feature in vowels and consonants.

It has been suggested that the proper measure for the feature of compactness would be somewhat akin to the measures of dispersion accepted in statistics. The usual measure for this is the second moment about the mean. Prelimin-ary calculations suggest this as a possible measure of compactness. Certain questions regarding the proper weighting of the frequency vs. intensity spec-trum remain open: especially whether a weighting like the equal loudness con-tour should be applied to the spectra before the moments are computed.

2.412 Production. The essential articulatory difference between the compact and diffuse phonemes lies in the relation between the volume of the resonating cavities in front of the narrowest stricture and those behind this stricture. The ratio of the former to the latter is higher for the compact than for the cor-responding diffuse phonemes.     Hence the consonants articulated against the hard or soft palate (velars and palatals) are more compact than the conso-nants articulated in the front part of the mouth. In the case of vowels the com-pactness increases with an increase in the cross-sectional area of any con-stricted passage. Thus open vowels are the most compact, while close vow-els are the most diffuse.

A higher ratio of the volume of the front to that of the back cavity can be also achieved by shortening the pharynx. This is the case in the production of compact consonants. In the corresponding diffuse consonants the pharyngeal cavity is lengthened by raising the velum and lowering the hyoid bone. X-ray photographs of the articulation of Finnish vowels and their measurements made by Sovijärvi are particularly revealing in this respect (13). The volume of the pharyngeal cavity for a diffuse phoneme is always bigger than for the corresponding (ceteris paribus) compact phoneme. (See Fig. 5).

2.413 Perception. Because of the higher over-all level usually associated with a longer duration, the compact phonemes display a higher "phonetic power" than the diffuse phonemes, ceteris paribus. Fletcher's calculations give the following "average values" ((14): table VIII, last column) for consonants of American English (and similar results for vowels):

| Compact | | Diffuse | | | |
|---------|------|------|-----|------|-----|
| /k/ | 3.0 | /t/ | 2.7 | /p/ | 1.0 |
| /g/ | 3.3 | /d/ | 1.7 | /b/ | 1.1 |
| /ʃ/ | 11.0 | /s/ | 0.9 | /f/ | 1.0 |
| /ŋ/ | 12.0 | /n/ | 4.1 | /m/ | 2.9 |

On the perceptual level a distinct association links the consonantal and vocalic opposition of compactness and diffuseness. As a recent experiment in Haskins laboratories (15) discloses, the same artificial "schematic stop was judged by a large majority of the subjects to be [p] when paired with [i] and [u], but to be [k] when paired with [a]". The contact with [a], the most compact, and with [i] and [u], the most diffuse of the vowels, prompts the association of this stop with [k], the most compact, and with [p], the most diffuse of the stops, respectively. Similarly the scale of magnitude, i.e. the small-vs.-large symbolism, latently connected for the average listeners with the opposition of compact and diffuse, works alike for vowels and for consonants (16).

The opposition compact vs. diffuse in the vowel pattern is the sole feature capable of presenting a middle term in addition to the two polar terms. On the perceptual level, experiments that obtained such middle terms through the mixture of a compact with the corresponding diffuse vowel (17) seem to confirm the peculiar structure of this vocalic feature, which sets it apart from all other inherent features.

2.414 Occurrence. The distinction of compact and diffuse vowels is apparrently universal. A few geographically scattered languages such as Tahitian and Kasimov-Tatar lack compact consonants (both velars and palatals). Often compact consonants occur only among stops, as in Danish.

But while consonants obey a strict dichotomy and may be either compact or diffuse, a parallel state in the vocalic pattern is frequent but not universal. E.g. in Roumanian (and similar relations exist in many other languages) the open /a/ and the close /ɨ/, as in rad "I shave" - rîd "I laugh", are opposed to one another as compact vs. diffuse. The corresponding mid vowel /ə/ is diffuse with respect to /a/ (cf. rắi "bad" - rai "paradise") but at the same time compact in relation to /ɨ/ (cf. vắr "cousin" - vîr "I introduce"). Thus compactness and diffuseness may be envisaged as two opposites, one symbolized by "plus" and the other by "minus": then /ə/ would be denoted by ±. This opposition of two contraries could, however, be resolved into two binary oppositions of contradictories: compact vs. non-compact and diffuse vs. non-diffuse. In this case, /ə/ would be doubly negative -- both non-compact and non-diffuse.

## 2.42 Tonality Features

This sub-class of the resonance features comprises three distinct dichotomous features capable of interacting variously with one another: a) the gravity feature, b) the flattening feature, and c) the sharpening feature.

## 2.421 Grave vs. Acute

2.4211 Stimulus. Acoustically this feature means the predominance of one side of the significant part of the spectrum over the other. When the lower side of the spectrum predominates, the phoneme is labeled grave; when the upper side predominates, we term the phoneme acute. Two measures suggest themselves as proper for this feature: a) the center of area, and b) the third moment about the center of area. As stated above (cf. 2.411), it is necessary before applying these criteria to normalize the spectra in some way. At present the proper normalizing function is still undetermined.

The great advantage of the third moment lies in the fact that here the predominance of the lower end of the spectrum would give negative values, while the predominance of the upper end would give positive values. Thus we could determine the gravity or acuteness of a sound without reference to any other standards. However, the fact that we must cube one of our variables (the frequency difference) seems to make the third moment an extremely sensitive measure which can only be used with extreme caution.

When using the center of area we avoid these difficulties, but at the same time we lose the advantages outlined above. The absolute values of the center of area cannot indicate whether a phoneme is grave or acute, for the center of area of an acute phoneme might well be lower than that of a grave; cf. the centers of area of the acute /e/ and the grave /f/ in the English word deaf. Thus it is impossible to decide whether a given phoneme is grave or acute without knowing at least some of the other features which the phoneme in question possesses.

Grave vs. acute vowels: Turkish /kɨs/ "malevolent" - /kis/ "tumor", /kus/ "vomit!" - /kys/ "reduce!"; /an/ "moment - /en/ "width", /on/ "ten" - /ɸn/ "front"

The position of the second formant in relation to that of the other formants in the spectrum is the most characteristic index of this feature: when it is closer to the first formant the phoneme is grave; when it is closer to the third and higher formants it is acute.

Grave vs. acute consonants: fill - sill, pill - till, bill - dill, mill - nil. In identifying the gravity feature of a consonant it is often profitable to observe the second formant in the adjacent vowel, if any: it is lowered in the case of grave consonants, and raised if the consonant is acute. This is the method advocated by Visible Speech (1). In some cases the position of the third and even higher formants may also be affected.

2.4212 Production. The gravity of a consonant or vowel is generated by a larger and less comparted mouth cavity, while acuteness originates in a smaller and more divided cavity. Hence gravity characterizes labial consonants as against dentals, as well as velars vs. palatals (see Fig. 5,) and, similarly, back vowels articulated with a retraction of the tongue vs. front vowels with advanced tongue (19).

Usually, however, a notable auxiliary factor in the formation of grave phonemes (back vowels and labial consonants as well as velars if opposed to palatals) is a contraction of the back orifice of the mouth resonator, through a narrowing of the pharynx, whereas the corresponding acute phonemes (dental and palatal consonants and front vowels) are produced with a widened pharynx. For instance, the widths of the cross-section of the pharyngeal cavity for the two classes of Czech consonants deviate from its width in silence (13.3 mm) as follows (measurements in mm):

| Grave | | Acute | |
|---|---|---|---|
| /u/ | - 3.8 | /i/ | + 15.2 |
| /o/ | - 5.5 | /e/ | + 4.0 |
| /f/ | - 4.7 | /s/ | + 6.3 |
| /x/ | - 3.8 | /ʃ/ | + 1.7 |
| /p/ | - 2.5 | /t/ | + 0.5 |
| /k/ | - 2.6 | /c/ | + 12.7 |
| /m/ | - 2.5 | /n/ | + 8.9 (See Fig. 5) |

## 2.422 Flat vs. Plain

### 2.4221 Stimulus.
Flattening manifests itself by a downward shift of a set of formants or even of all the formants in the spectrum.

Flat vs. plain vowels: Turkish /kus/ - /k<del>i</del>s/, /kys/ - /kis/; /on/ - /an/; /ǿn/ - /en/ (See Fig. 4). We employ a conventional musical term for labeling this feature, and in phonemic transcription we may correspondingly use a subscript or superscript musical flat "♭" to denote the flat consonants. Examples from Rutulian, a North Caucasian language: /iak/ "light" - /iak/ "flesh" /X̌ar/ "more" - /X̌ar/ "hail". (See Fig. 6). ♭

### 2.4222 Production.
Flattening is chiefly generated by a reduction of the lip orifice (rounding) with a concomitant increase in the length of the lip constriction. Hence the opposition flat vs. plain has been genetically termed "orifice variation", and the opposition grave vs. acute "cavity variation" (18).

Instead of the front orifice of the mouth cavity, the pharyngeal tract, in its turn, may be contracted with a similar effect of flattening (20). This independent pharyngeal contraction, called pharyngealization, affects the acute consonants and attenuates their acuteness (See Fig. 7). The fact that peoples who have no pharyngealized consonants in their mother tongue, as, for instance, the Bantus and the Uzbeks, substitute labialized articulations for the corresponding pharyngealized consonants of Arabic words, illustrates the perceptual similarity of pharyngealization and lip-rounding. These two processes do not occur within one language. Hence they are to be treated as two variants of a single opposition-flat vs. plain. The two phonetic signs [t̰] and [ɫ] used for rounded and pharyngealized consonants respectively could be replaced by a single symbol in the phonemic transcription. The subscript or superscript musical flat which we have employed for the Caucasian rounded consonants can also be used for the Arabic pharyngealized consonants: /dirs/ "molar" - /dirs/ "camel's tail", /salb/ "crucifixion" -/salb/ "despoiling."

On the autonomous use of the "back orifice variation" for the grave consonants and for the vowels see 2.4236.

## 2.423 Sharp vs. Plain

### 2.4231 Stimulus.
This feature manifests itself in a slight rise of the second formant and, to some degree, also of the higher formants.

Examples: Russian /m̥'at/ "to rumple" - /m'at/ "rumpled" - /m'at̮/ "mother" - /m'at/ "checkmate", /kr'of/ "blood" - /kr'of/ "shelter" (see Fig. 9).

### 2.4232 Production.
To effect this feature, the oral cavity is reduced by raising a part of the tongue against the palate. This adjustment, called pala-

talization, is made simultaneously with the main articulation of a given consonant and is linked with a greater dilatation of the pharyngeal pass in comparison with the corresponding plain consonant. The pharyngeal dilatation of the plain acute consonants is further augmented for the sharpened ones. The pharyngeal contraction of the plain grave consonants is supplanted by a dilation for the sharpened ones (see Fig. 9). Hence the behavior of the pharynx is particularly important in the sharpening of the grave consonants and may, under certain circumstances, become its main factor (see 2.4236).

2.4233 Perception of Tonality Features. The intelligibility of acute phonemes is seriously impaired by the elimination of their high frequencies, while the grave phonemes are hardly recognizable when losing the low frequencies (21 and 14). A schematic stop is perceived as [t] when endowed with distinctly higher frequencies and as [p] when endowed with distinctly low frequencies (cf. 2.413).

Two phonemes contrasted as grave and acute (e.g., /u/ vs. /y/ or /ɨ/ vs. /i/ or /f/ vs. /s/) are easily identified as dark and light respectively by responsive subjects synesthetically oriented, while the contrast of flat and plain, /u/ vs. /ɨ/ or /y/ vs. /i/, produces rather a sensation of depth, breadth, weight and bluntness vs. thinness, height, lightness and shrillness. A closer study of these two dimensions of auditory sensation in their relation to the distinct acoustic stimuli and to the reactions of the same listeners upon the compactness feature could contribute to the elucidation and delimitation of the different sound attributes.

The increased "corpulence" and "hardness" ascribed by the Arabic grammatical tradition to the pharyngealized consonants in terms of auditory experience is similarly applied by Caucasian observers to the rounded consonants.

The sharpened acute consonants as /ș/, /ț/ are sensed by responsive subjects as slightly brighter than /s/, /t/ and the sharpened grave /f̦/, /p̦/ as somewhat less dark than /f/, /p/.

Subjects endowed with colored hearing refer to vowels as chromatic and to consonants as achromatic, grayish. The contrast between acute and grave phonemes is correlated with the white-black, yellow-blue and green-red responses, whereas compact phonemes are prevalently matched with the colors at the greatest distance from the white-black axis (22). Experiments in vowel mixing show that grave and acute vowels when sounded simultaneously are not perceived as a single vowel (17). This test may be compared to a similar experience with colors - the non-existence of bluish yellow or reddish green (23).

2.4234 Occurrence of Tonality Features. Each language presents at least one tonality feature. We term it primary. Moreover, a language may contain one or two secondary tonality features.

2.4235 The Primary Tonality Feature. Consonants almost universally possess a tonality feature. As a rule, the diffuse consonants exhibit the opposition grave vs. acute, which often is found also in the compact consonants. In other words, the consonant patterns usually include both labial and dental phonemes and frequently also mutually opposed velars and palatals. Such is, for instance, the case in several Central European languages - Czech, Slovak, Serbocroatian and Hungarian. Their consonant phonemes form a square pattern, while in languages such as English and French,which do not split their compact consonants into grave and,ceteris paribus,acute phonemes, this pattern is triangular:

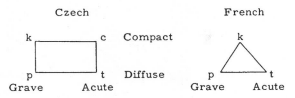

In the few American and African languages that have no labials, their absence, for the most part, can be traced to the traditional use of labrets. Moreover, most of these rare consonant patterns, devoid of the opposition grave vs. acute, have another tonality feature: flat vs. plain; e.g. Tlingit (Alaska), Iroquoian, and Wichita (Oklahoma); cf. such Tlingit word-pairs as [jaːk̲]"canoe"-[jaːk] "shell".

In vowel patterns with only one tonality feature, the following three cases are found: a) the opposition grave vs. acute alone; b) rarely, the opposition flat vs. plain alone; c) quite frequently, a fusion of the two oppositions. Examples for the first kind are Wichita (24) and Slovak, with such pairs as Slovak mat' /mac/ "mother" - mät' /mæc/"mint", or Japanese, where the grave phoneme opposed to /i/ is produced without lip-rounding. In Russian, which exemplifies the second type, close phonemes /u/ and /i/ are opposed to each other only as flat (rounded)to plain (unrounded), because in certain positions both of these phonemes are represented by front variants and in certain others by back variants: [ʃyɟ'it] "to play pranks" -[ʃiɟ'it] "to smoke", [rv'u] "I tear" - [rv'ɨ] "moats". In these cases only one of the two processes is phonemically relevant, while the other is a redundant feature appearing only in certain definite phonemic contexts. The third type, an indissoluble fusion of both processes, takes place in Spanish and Italian: e.g. Spanish /puso/ "he put" - /piso/ "tread", /poso/ "sediment" - /peso/ "weight". Here in the opposition grave vs. acute a wide undivided mouth cavity is always accompanied by rounding, while a smaller and more comparted cavity is never accompanied by rounding. Thus in these patterns only the optimal grave and the optimal acute are opposed to each other.

If there is only one tonality feature in the vowels of a given language,then it may be lumped with the primary (or only) tonality feature of the consonants, regardless of which of the three above patterns actually occurs. For example, Russian uses one opposition (flat vs. plain) as the only tonality feature in the vowels, and another (grave vs. acute) as the primary tonality feature in the consonants. The difference between these features is, however, redundant since it accompanies the opposition of vowels vs. consonants, and consequently the only relevant factor here is the common denominator of the two tonality features.

The sole or primary tonality feature is often confined to diffuse vowels. Hence vowels, like consonants, form either a square or a triangular pattern:

2.4236 The Secondary Tonality Features. In a number of languages the consonants use the opposition flat vs. plain as a secondary feature, in addition to the primary feature, i.e. the opposition grave vs. acute. Flattening produced by lip-rounding is wide-spread in the Caucasus and also occurs in some native languages of Asia, Africa and America. It mainly affects velars, but is sometimes extended to other consonants as well. Another variety of flattened phonemes, the pharyngealized (so-called emphatic) consonants appear in some Semitic and adjacent languages. This process affects the diffuse acute (dental) consonants and attenuates their acuteness, while in the compact consonants it fuses with the primary opposition grave vs. acute and intensifies the distinction between palatals and velars by imposing upon the latter a very strong pharyngeal contraction.

The distinction of retroflex and dental consonants, characteristic in particular of various languages in India, is another manifestation of the same opposition (see Fig. 8): both the contraction of the pharynx and the elongation of the resonating cavity take place in producing emphatic as well as retroflex consonants, but for the former the first process, and for the latter the second one seems to be of greater pertinence.

Liquids and glides, also, undergo either rounding or pharyngealization and may partake in the opposition flat vs. plain. Thus Circassian distinguishes a rounded and unrounded glottal catch: / ʔ a/ "say!" - / ʔ a/ "hand". Arabic has an aspiration with and without contraction of the pharynx: /ḥadam/ "it was hot" - /hadam/ "he pulled down", /jaḥdim/ "it is hot" - /jaḥdim/ "he pulls down".

The opposition of sharpened and plain consonants plays an important part, e.g., in Gaelic, Roumanian, Polish, Russian and several languages adjacent to the latter. It primarily affects the diffuse acute consonants (dentals), but is sometimes extended also to other classes (labials and velars).

In a few languages rounded (flat) and palatalized (sharp) consonants may co-exist, e.g. the Abkhazian language in the Caucasus opposes a plain phoneme as /g/ to the corresponding flat /g̦/, on the one hand, and to the sharpened /g̗/, on the other. In single languages such as Dungan Chinese and Kashmiri, the two co-existing oppositions realize all four possible combinations: 1) rounded unpalatalized, 2) unrounded unpalatalized, 3) rounded palatalized, 4) unrounded palatalized. (Cf. the vowel series /u/ - /i/ - /y/ - /i/). E.g. Kashmiri distinguishes in this manner four different grammatical forms of the verb "to do": /kar̗/ - /kar/ - /kaɹ/ - /kaɹ̗/. In the rounded palatalized phonemes the second formant moves closer to the third while at the same time all formants are moved down in frequency.

Finally the combination of flats and sharps within one language can acquire another form. Beside languages such as Arabic, which confine the autonomous role of the pharynx to its contraction for the flattening of the acute consonants, there are a few languages in the NE Caucasus which employ the widening of the pharynx to sharpen the grave consonants. This is the essence of the so-called "emphatic softening" (25). Both these processes - the flattening of the acuteness and the sharpening of the gravity - may be reduced to a common denominator: the attenuation of the primary feature through a pharyngeal modification. Consequently we may transcribe the dentals with narrowed pharynx in one and the same way. Examples from Lakkian (NE Caucasus): /d̦a: / "middle" - /da:/ "come", and /m̈a/ "bolt" - /ma/ "have it.".

In a great number of languages each of the two oppositions - grave vs. acute and flat vs. plain - acts separately in the vowel pattern. If in such a language two vowel phonemes are opposed to each other by contrary positions of their second formant, then at least one of these two phonemes is at the same time opposed to a third phoneme by a shift in the first three formants and in some of the higher formants. Thus French (and similarly Scandinavian languages, standard German, and Hungarian) distinguishes two classes of acute vowels and one - an optimal class - of grave vowels: plain acute - flat acute - flat grave: nid /ni/ "nest" - nu /ny/ "naked" - nous /nu/ "we".

Other languages, e.g. Roumanian and Ukranian, have two classes of grave vowels - flat as /u/, plain as /i/ - and only a single, optimal class of acute vowels - plain as /i/. A comparable distribution appears in the variety of English described by D. Jones (RP). Diffuse vowels: acute in pit /p'it/ - plain grave in putt /p'ət/ - flat grave in put /p'ut/; compact vowels: acute in pet /p'et/ - plain grave in pat /p'at/ - flat grave in pot /p'ot/. It is true that in pat the contextual variant representing the phoneme /a/ is the front [æ], but the tongue' in producing this English vowel is more retracted than in producing acute vowels, and moreover a pharyngeal contraction "appears to be an inherent characteristic of the sound", as noted by D. Jones and other observers. This connects it with the back variant of the same phoneme and with the other grave vowels.

Finally in Turkish both the grave and the acute vowels are split into two opposite sub-classes - flat and plain: /kus/ - /kis/ - /kys/ - /kis/; /on/ - /an/ -

/ø̷n/ - /en/. Cf. the diagram:

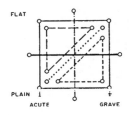

When a language possesses only three classes of vowels: an optimal grave, an optimal acute and an attenuated class, i.e. either flat acute or plain grave, then, as far as the structure of the vowel pattern does not prevent it, it is possible to interpret all three classes in terms of one opposition. With this assumption, /u/ is "+", /i/ is "-" and /y/ or /ɨ/ is "+" vs. /i/, but "-" vs. /u/ and hence may be symbolized by "±". The opposition flat vs. plain as a secondary tonality feature of vowels supplements the optimal grave vs. acute opposition by an attenuated grave and/or acute; for instance /u/ and /i/ by /ɨ/ and/or /y/. In a few Caucasian, Nilotic and Hindu languages, a similar attenuation is performed by a dilation of the pharynx (sharpening) for the grave vowels and its contraction (flattening) for the acute vowels. This pharyngeal behavior generates two series of centralized vowels opposed to the back and front vowels respectively, e.g., in Dinka (Anglo-Egyptian Sudan) /ü/ - /u/, /ö/ - /o/; /ï/ - /i/, /ë/ - /e/: /dit/ "bird" - /dit/ "big".

### 2.43 Tense vs. Lax

2.431 Stimulus. In contradistinction to the lax phonemes the corresponding tense phonemes display a longer sound interval and a larger energy (defined as the area under the envelope of the sound intensity curve; cf. 2.31).

In a tense vowel the sum of the deviation of its formants from the neutral position is greater than that of the corresponding lax vowel (cf. 2.13). A similar deviation may be presumed for the spectrum of the tense consonants (called strong or fortes) in comparison with their lax counterparts (called weak or lenes).

In consonants, tenseness is manifested primarily by the length of their sounding period, and in stops, in addition, by the greater strength of the explosion.

The opposition of tense and lax vowels has often been confused with the distinction between more diffuse and more compact vowels and with the corresponding articulatory difference between higher and lower tongue position. But the more diffuse vowels are, ceteris paribus, shorter than the more compact, whereas the tense vowels have a longer duration than the corresponding lax.

Examples. Tense vs. lax consonants: English pill - bill, till - dill, kill - gill /gil/, chill - gill /ʒil/, fill - vill, sip - zip. Tense vs. lax vowels: French saute /sot/ "jump" - sotte /sot/ "fool" (fem.), pâte /pɑt/ "paste" - patte /pat/ "paw", las /la/ "tired" - là /la/ "there", jeûne /ʒøn/ "fast" - jeune /ʒœn/ "young", tête /tɛt/ "head" - tette /tet/ "suckle", thé /te/ "tea" - taie /tɛ/ "pillow case" (the difference in duration which is crucial for the distinction between /e/ and /ɛ/ before consonants is notably reduced at the end of the word).

## French Tense and Lax Vowels

| | $F_1$ | $F_2$ | $F_3$ | $\Sigma \triangle f$ |
|---|---|---|---|---|
| Neutral Position (Mlle. D.) | 570 | 1710 | 2850 | |
| saute /sot/ | 480 | 1000 | 2850 | |
| $\triangle f$ | 90 | 710 | 0 | 800 |
| sotte /sot/ | 520 | 1400 | 3000 | |
| $\triangle f$ | 50 | 310 | 150 | 510 |
| pâte /pɑt/ | 600 | 1200 | 2800 | |
| $\triangle f$ | 30 | 510 | 50 | 590 |
| patte /pat/ | 650 | 1600 | 2650 | |
| $\triangle f$ | 80 | 110 | 200 | 390 |
| tête /tɛt/ | 600 | 2100 | 3200 | |
| $\triangle f$ | 30 | 390 | 350 | 770 |
| tette /tet/ | 600 | 1900 | 2500 | |
| $\triangle f$ | 30 | 190 | 350 | 570 |
| thé /te/ | 450 | 2300 | 3200 | |
| $\triangle f$ | 120 | 590 | 350 | 1070 |
| taie /te/ | 600 | 2100 | 2650 | |
| $\triangle f$ | 30 | 390 | 200 | 620 |

The sum of the deviations of the formants of a tense vowel is always greater than that of the corresponding lax vowel. Tense vowels are usually considerably longer than the corresponding lax vowels (32).

2.432 Production. Tense phonemes are articulated with greater distinctness and pressure than the corresponding lax phonemes. The muscular strain affects the tongue, the walls of the vocal tract and the glottis. The higher tension is associated with a greater deformation of the entire vocal tract from its neutral position. This is in agreement with the fact that tense phonemes have a longer duration than their lax counterparts. The acoustic effects due to the greater and less rigidity of the walls remain open to question.

2.433 Perception. Rousselot's (26) and Fletcher's (14) tests have shown that ceteris paribus, tense phonemes possess a higher audibility than the corresponding lax phonemes. For English consonants, Fletcher (Table IX) gives the following data on the number of decibels by which single sounds must be attenuated in order to render them inaudible.

| | | | | | |
|---|---|---|---|---|---|
| Tense: | k 83.8 | t 84.1 | p 80.6 | s 82.4 | f 83.6 |
| Lax: | g 82.9 | d 78.9 | b 78.8 | z 81.6 | v 81.4 |

The importance of the difference in the duration for the distinction of tense and lax consonants is illustrated by the experiments of L. G. Jones: when the beginnings of $\lceil p \rceil$, $\lceil t \rceil$, $\lceil k \rceil$ (originally produced by cutting the corresponding constrictives, cf. 2.3113) had been erased on tape recordings, they were apprehended by native English listeners as $\lceil b \rceil$, $\lceil d \rceil$, $\lceil g \rceil$. Slavic listeners, however, still heard $\lceil p \rceil$, $\lceil t \rceil$, $\lceil k \rceil$, since not the tenseness but the voicing feature is relevant for them (see 2.434).

2.434 Occurrence. In many languages, e.g. Cantonese, the consonant phonemes display neither of the two oppositions, voiced vs. voiceless and lax vs. tense.

In a number of languages only one of these two oppositions is relevant. If the opposition of tense and lax consonants is the only distinctive one, then either none of them are voiced, as, for instance, in Danish, or voicing and voicelessness become concomitant factors of laxness and tenseness respectively, as in English or French. In such languages the tenseness feature is more constant than the redundant voicing feature. This hierarchy is illustrated, for instance, by the French pattern, where $[ʒ]$, the voiced lax (lenis) consonant of such forms as tu la jettes, becomes a voiceless lax $[ʒ̥]$ before the voiceless $[t]$ in vous la jetez but is still distinguished from $[ʃ]$, the voiceless tense (fortis), in vous l'achetez. In some of these languages the tense stops are aspirated either generally, or, as in English, the aspiration is confined to certain positions.

The inverse relation is observable, e.g. in Slavic languages, where the voicing feature is the relevant one, while the tenseness feature is only concomitant and optional to a certain degree.

Finally, there is a relatively limited number of languages where both of these oppositions are present in the phonemic pattern. In this case the autonomous opposition voiced vs. voiceless is ordinarily confined to the stops; the aspiration is used to implement the opposition of tense and lax stops, and, for the most part, only the unvoiced stops are split into aspirated and non-aspirated; e.g. Suto (South Africa): /dula/ "sit" - /tula/ "crack" - /thula/ "to butt" (27). Seldom, especially in a few Indic languages, the voiced class, too, presents pairs of tense and lax stops (aspirated and unaspirated respectively). Conversely, in some languages of the Caucasus, which distinguish voiced, checked, lax and tense stops (e.g. in Lezgian and Ossete), the redundant feature of aspiration marks the lax stops in contradistinction to the tense.

The prevocalic or postvocalic aspiration /h/ is opposed to the even, unaspirated onset or decay of a vowel. The former is a tense glide (spiritus asper), and the latter, a lax glide (spiritus lenis), which properly speaking is a zero phoneme. This opposition (/h/ - /#/) occurs in English in initial prevocalic position:
hill:ill~pill:bill; hue /hi'uu/: you / i'uu/ ≃ tune / ti'uun/: dune / di'uun/. The lax counterpart of /h/ presents an optional variant: in cases of emphasis a glottal catch may be substituted for the even onset: an aim can appear in the form [ən?'eim] in order to be clearly distinguished from a name [ən'eim]. Ordinarily languages which possess an opposition of tense and lax consonants have an /h/ phoneme too.

An example of the opposition tense vs. lax in liquids is presented by the strongly rolled and flapped /r/ in Spanish: tense in perro "dog" - lax in pero "but".

The opposition of tense and lax vowels occurs in various regions of the world: sometimes it encompasses the entire vocalic pattern, but most often it affects only some of the vowel phonemes, as in Italian with its two pairs of tense and lax vowels, e.g. /tọrta/ "tart" -/torta/ "crooked" (fem.), /pesca/ "fishing" - /pesca/ "peach".

### 2.44 Supplementary Resonator: Nasal vs. Oral

2.441 Stimulus.    The nasalization feature may pertain both to consonants and to vowels: English din - did, dim - dib, ding /diŋ/ - dig; French banc [bã] "bench" - bas[ba]"low".

The spectrum of the nasal phonemes shows a higher formant density than that of the corresponding oral phonemes (see Fig. 11). According to M. Joos (28) between the first and the second vowel formants there appears in the nasal vowels an additional formant with concomitant weakening in the intensity of the former two. In vowels like /a/ with a high first formant the additional nasal formant appears below, rather than above, the lowest formant of the corresponding oral vowel.

The nasal consonants add to the corresponding oral stops (/m/ to /b/, /n/ to /d/, /ŋ/ to /g/, and /ɲ/ to /ɟ/) a nasal murmur throughout their closure period. In addition to several variable formants, this murmur possesses two constant and clear formants, one at about 200 cps. and the other at about 2500 cps.

The formants in the murmur part are relatively stable: in the spectrogram they appear as straight horizontal lines, and the transitions to and from the adjacent phoneme are usually quite abrupt.

The additional poles and zeros, due to nasalization, are a local distortion in the spectrum without any influence on the other resonance features. These fundamental features are determined solely by the original set of non-nasal poles which affect the entire spectrum.*

2.442 Production. The oral (or more exactly, the non-nasalized) phonemes are formed by the air stream which escapes from the larynx through the mouth cavity only. The nasal (or more exactly, nasalized) phonemes are, on the contrary, produced with a lowering of the soft palate, so that the air stream is bifurcated and the mouth resonator is supplemented by the nasal cavity.

2.443 Occurrence. The opposition oral vs. nasal is nearly universal in consonant patterns, with isolated exceptions such as Wichita (24). But a great number of languages have no distinction of nasal vs. oral vowels. The number of nasal phonemes in the vowel and consonant pattern is never higher, and usually lower, than the number of oral phonemes. Nasality can be combined with other resonance features, and with rare exceptions at least two nasal consonants are distinguished - the diffuse acute /n/ and the diffuse grave /m/. Frequently there is, in addition, one compact nasal; rarely, two: one acute /ɲ/ and the other grave /ŋ/. In respect to the voicing feature the nasal consonants behave like liquids; normally they are voiced and seldom partake of the opposition voiced vs. voiceless: cf. Kuanyama (SW Africa): /na/ "with" - /na̬/ "quite" (27). Other consonantal source features are also very rare in nasals.

## 2.5 CONCLUSION

The inherent distinctive features which we detect in the languages of the world and which underlie their entire lexical and morphological stock amount to twelve binary oppositions: 1) vocalic/non-vocalic, 2) consonantal/non-consonantal, 3) interrupted/continuant, 4) checked/unchecked, 5) strident/mellow, 6) voiced/unvoiced, 7) compact/diffuse, 8) grave/acute, 9) flat/plain, 10) sharp/plain, 11) tense/lax, 12) nasal/oral.

No language contains all of these features. Their joint occurrence or incompatibility both within the same language and within the same phoneme is to a

---

* John Lotz has made the following suggestion: "There are vowels which are not nasal and there are vowels which are nasal and consequently show a consonantal disruption of the vocalic pattern. But the nasal quality is clearly superposed, since it can only function in addition to another quality. In general terms, if a feature is implied - and in the hierarchy secondary - we subtract it from the total wave and thus obtain the basic phenomenon."

considerable extent determined by laws of implication which are universally valid or at least have a high statistical probability: X implies the presence of Y and/or the absence of Z. These laws exhibit the stratification of the phonemic patterns and reduce their apparent variety to a limited set of structural types.

Despite their multiform interdependence within the phoneme and within the entire phonemic pattern, the different distinctive features remain autonomous. Not only may any feature perform its distinctive function (/gip/≠ /gib/≠/gid/), but the identification of a single feature regardless of the different phonemes in which it occurs is seen to play a significant part in language.

The autonomy of various distinctive features clearly comes to light in the grammatical process known in certain languages under the name of <u>vowel harmony</u>. In such languages a word-unit is limited in the choice of its vocalic features. Thus in some languages of the Far East the vowels of a word unit must be either all compact or all diffuse, e.g. in Gold (on the Amur) it may contain either only /o a e/ or only /u ə i/: /gepalego/ "liberate" - /gisurəgu/"re-tell".

In Finnish those acute vowels which <u>ceteris paribus</u> are paired with grave vowels cannot belong to the same simple word-unit as the grave vowels. The Finnish vowel pattern includes:

|  | Flat |  | Plain |  |
|---|---|---|---|---|
|  | Grave | Acute | Grave | Acute |
|  |  |  | a | æ |
|  | o | ø |  | e |
|  | u | y |  | i |

Hence a word unit may contain either / a o u/ or / æ ø y/, while the plain acute vowels / e i/, which have no plain grave correspondents, are combinable with any Finnish vowel.

In most of the Turkic languages, grave and acute vowels are incompatible within a word unit; and to a greater or lesser extent the same device is applied to the flat and plain vowels. E.g., in Turkish:

| Root-vowels | Suffix "our" |
|---|---|
| flat grave | /-muz/ |
| plain  " | /-mɨz/ |
| flat acute | /-myz/ |
| plain  " | /-miz/ |

Ibo (S. Nigeria) has eight vowel phonemes displaying three oppositions: compact vs. diffuse, grave vs. acute, and tense vs. lax. A root contains either only tense /o̞ e̞ u̞ i̞/ or only lax vowels /o e u i/.

A "consonant harmony" has been developed by the language of the NW Karaites (in Lithuania): the consonants of a word unit are either all sharp or all plain; e.g. /k̦un̦lar̦dan̦/ "from days" - /kunlardan/ "from servants".

An extraction of the consonantal compactness and gravity features achieved by an extinction of all other consonantal features is documented by the conventional consonant mutilations in the diction of the Pima songs (SW America) recorded and analyzed by George Herzog.

Voicing is the only consonantal feature relevant for the Slavic assonances (22). For example, Polish oral and written poetry, when using assonances, takes as equivalent all voiced (doba - droga - woda - koza - sowa) and similarly all unvoiced consonants (kopa - sroka - rota - rosa - sofa), while the pairing of voiced and unvoiced consonants is inadmissible. The fact that the words /rota/ "company" and /rosa/ "dew" are semantically distinguished by one feature (interrupted vs. continuant) and at the same time equated in assonance by another feature of the same phoneme (voicelessness) is striking testimony for the operational autonomy of the distinctive features.

# APPENDIX

## Analytic Transcription

The phonemes may be broken down into the inherent distinctive features which are the ultimate discrete signals. Were this operation reduced to yes-or-no situations, the phoneme pattern of English (Received Pronunciation) could be presented as follows:

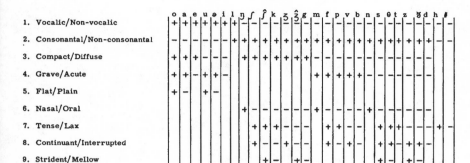

| | o | a | e | u | ə | i | l | ŋ | ʃ | ʃ̂ | k | ʒ | ʒ̂ | g | m | f | p | v | b | n | s | θ | t | z | ð | d | h | # |
|---|---|---|---|---|---|---|---|---|---|---|---|---|---|---|---|---|---|---|---|---|---|---|---|---|---|---|---|---|
| 1. Vocalic/Non-vocalic | + | + | + | + | + | + | − | − | − | − | − | − | − | − | − | − | − | − | − | − | − | − | − | − | − | − | − | − |
| 2. Consonantal/Non-consonantal | − | − | − | − | − | − | + | + | + | + | + | + | + | + | + | + | + | + | + | + | + | + | + | + | + | + | − | − |
| 3. Compact/Diffuse | + | + | + | − | − | − | | + | + | + | + | + | + | + | − | − | − | − | − | − | − | − | − | − | − | − | | |
| 4. Grave/Acute | + | + | − | + | + | − | | + | − | − | + | − | − | + | | | | | | | | | | | | | | |
| 5. Flat/Plain | + | − | | + | − | | | | | | | | | | | | | | | | | | | | | | | |
| 6. Nasal/Oral | | | | | | | | + | − | − | − | − | − | − | + | − | − | − | − | + | | | | | | | | |
| 7. Tense/Lax | | | | | | | | | + | + | + | − | − | − | | + | + | − | − | | + | + | + | − | − | − | + | − |
| 8. Continuant/Interrupted | | | | | | | | | + | − | − | + | − | − | | + | − | + | − | | + | + | − | + | + | − | | |
| 9. Strident/Mellow | | | | | | | | | | + | − | | | | | + | − | | | | + | − | | | | | | |

Key to phonemic transcription: /o/ - pot, /a/ - pat; /e/ - pet, /u/ - put, /ə/ - putt, /i/ - pit, /l/ - lull, /ŋ/ - lung, /ʃ/ - ship, /ʃ̂/ - chip, /k/ - kip, /ʒ/ - azure, /ʒ̂/ - juice, /g/ - goose, /m/ - mill, /f/ - fill, /p/ - pill, /v/ - vim, /b/ - bill, /n/ - nil, /s/ - sill, /θ/ - thill, /t/ - till, /z/ - zip, /ð/ - this, /d/ - dill, /h/ - hill, /#/ - ill. The prosodic opposition stressed vs. unstressed, splits each of the vowel phonemes into two.

The superposition of the distinctive features in the given language - in this instance English - determines their order in our analytic transcription.

I) The identification of the fundamental source features (1,2) divides the components of the message into vowels, consonants, glides and a liquid, whereby the latter does not demand further analysis.

II) The superposition of resonance features in vowels and consonants presents the following order: A) the compactness feature (3) encompasses all vowels and consonants; B) the gravity feature (4) concerns all vowels and compact consonants whereby the analysis of the acute vowels is exhausted; C) the flattening feature (5) is confined to grave vowels and terminates their analysis, while D) the nasality feature (6) affects uniquely the consonants and concludes the identification of the nasals; finally the tenseness feature (7) concerns all phonemes without a vocalic and nasal feature, i.e. the oral consonants and the glides.

III) The secondary source features (8, 9) characterize the oral consonants alone.*

When, however, the analytic transcription of the English phonemes is intended to determine the amount of significant information the phonemes actually carry in linguistic communication, it is expedient to distinguish the unpredictable from the predictable, consequently, redundant features by bracketing the latter. Furthermore, the entire list of features can be reduced, if we acknowledge the joint presence of two opposite features (±) in one phoneme. Then the same pattern of English may be compressed as follows:

| | o | a | e | u | ə | i | l | ŋ | ʃ | ĵ | k | ʒ | ẑ | g | m | f | p | v | b | n | s | θ | t | z | ð | d | h | (#) |
|---|---|---|---|---|---|---|---|---|---|---|---|---|---|---|---|---|---|---|---|---|---|---|---|---|---|---|---|---|
| Vocalic/Consonantal | + | + | + | + | + | + | ± | (−) | (−) | (−) | (−) | (−) | (−) | (−) | (−) | (−) | (−) | (−) | (−) | (−) | (−) | (−) | (−) | (−) | (−) | (−) | | |
| Compact/Diffuse | + | + | + | − | − | − | | + | + | + | + | + | + | + | | | | | | (−) | (−) | (−) | (−) | (−) | (−) | (−) | (−) | (−) |
| Grave/Acute | + | ± | − | + | ± | − | | | | | | | | | + | + | + | + | + | − | − | − | − | − | − | − | | |
| Nasal/Oral | | | | | | | | (−) | (−) | (−) | (−) | (−) | | + | (−) | (−) | (−) | (−) | + | (−) | (−) | (−) | (−) | (−) | (−) | + | (−) | |
| Tense/Lax | | | | | | | | + | + | + | − | − | − | | + | + | − | | + | + | + | − | | + | + | − | | |
| Optimal Constrictive/ Opt. Stop | | | | | | | | + | ± | − | + | ± | − | | + | − | + | − | | + | ± | − | + | ± | − | | | |

The phonemes of the famous test sentence, "Joe took father's shoe bench out; she was waiting at my lawn", will be analytically transcribed as follows:

| | ẑ | o | u | t | ʼu | k | f | ʼa | ə | ð | ə | z | ʃ | ʼu | u | b | ʼe | n | ʃ | # | ʼa | u | t |
|---|---|---|---|---|---|---|---|---|---|---|---|---|---|---|---|---|---|---|---|---|---|---|---|
| Vocalic | (−) | + | + | (−) | + | (−) | (−) | + | + | (−) | + | (−) | (−) | + | + | (−) | + | (−) | (−) | | + | + | (−) |
| Compact | + | + | − | (−) | − | + | (−) | + | | − | (−) | − | (−) | + | − | − | (−) | + | (−) | + | | + | − | (−) |
| Grave | | + | + | | − | + | + | ± | ± | − | ± | − | | + | + | | − | − | | | ± | + | − |
| Nasal | (−) | | | (−) | | (−) | (−) | | | (−) | | (−) | (−) | | | (−) | | + | (−) | | | | (−) |
| Tense | − | | | + | | + | + | | − | | − | | + | | | − | | | + | (−) | | | + |
| Optimal Constrictive | ± | | | − | | − | + | | ± | | + | | + | | | − | | | ± | | | | − |
| Stressed | + | | − | | + | | + | | − | | − | | + | | − | | + | | | | + | | − |

| | ʃ | ʼi | i | u | ʼə | z | u | ʼe | i | t | i | ŋ | # | ə | t | m | ʼa | i | l | ʼo | ə | n |
|---|---|---|---|---|---|---|---|---|---|---|---|---|---|---|---|---|---|---|---|---|---|---|
| Vocalic | (−) | + | + | + | + | (−) | + | + | + | (−) | + | (−) | | + | (−) | (−) | + | + | ± | + | + | (−) |
| Compact | + | − | − | − | − | (−) | − | + | − | (−) | − | + | | − | (−) | (−) | + | − | | + | − | (−) |
| Grave | | − | − | + | ± | − | + | − | − | − | − | − | | ± | − | + | ± | − | | + | ± | − |
| Nasal | (−) | | | | | (−) | | | | (−) | | + | | (−) | | + | | | | | | + |
| Tense | + | | | | − | | | + | | | | + | | + | | | | | | | | |
| Optimal Constrictive | + | | | | + | | | − | | | | − | | − | | | | | | | | |
| Stressed | + | | − | − | + | | − | + | − | | − | | | − | | | + | − | | + | − | |

By omitting the features fully predictable from the phonemic environment, we could further reduce the amount of redundancy in our analytic transcription. For example, in English, /ʼa/ cannot be followed by a compact vowel, and the second component in the sequences /ʼau/ or /ʼai/ is distinctly characterized by the opposition grave vs. acute. Consequently the diffuseness of /u/ and /i/

*For mechanical detection the procedural sequence should be modified as follows: features 6, 8 and 9 must be determined before features 3, 4, 5.

- 44 -

in these combinations is redundant and can be omitted in the transcription. If we consistently follow this principle by bracketing any feature predictable from other features of the same phoneme or from other phonemes of the same sequence, the amount of actually distinctive features in a sequence proves to be very restricted. For instance, in the Russian word <u>velosiped</u> "velocipede, bicycle," if analyzed in this way almost half the features present appear as redundant, so that the average amount of non-redundant features approximates 3 per phoneme.

| | γ | i | l | a | ş | i | p | 'e | t |
|---|---|---|---|---|---|---|---|---|---|
| Vocalic/Consonantal | (−) | + | ± | + | (−) | + | (−) | (+) | (−) |
| Compact/Diffuse | (−) | (−) | | + | (−) | (−) | − | ± | − |
| Grave/Acute | + | (−) | | − | − | | + | − | − |
| Nasal/Oral | (−) | | | | (−) | | (−) | | (−) |
| Sharp/Plain | + | | (−) | | + | | (+) | | − |
| Continuant/Interrupted | + | | + | | + | | − | | − |
| Voiced/Voiceless | + | | | | − | | − | | (−) |
| Stressed/Unstressed | | (−) | | (−) | | (−) | | (+) | |

A few remarks will suffice to expose the reasons for our bracketing. No unstressed /e/ exists in Russian, consequently here the stress feature turns out to be redundant. Since a Russian word carries not more than one stressed vowel, in our word all vowels other than /e/ must be unstressed (second degree of redundancy). After /γ/ the only possible unstressed vowel is /i/, so that the diffuseness and acuteness of this phoneme is a third degree of redundancy. Here the consonant cancels certain features of the vowel which follows. The subsequent syllable exemplifies the inverse process: The vowel cancels certain features of the consonant which precedes. After a plain /l/, the unstressed vowel may be either compact or diffuse, and, if diffuse, either grave or acute, but before the unstressed /a/ no sharp /l/ is possible. Consequently in this case, the lack of sharpening is redundant, in the same way as its presence before /e/, e.g. the sharpened stop in the syllable /p'et/.

A further extraction of redundancies can be achieved by taking account of probabilities less than one, which were disregarded in the preceding. The mathematical techniques for such an undertaking are in a very advanced stage of development owing to the researches of A. A. Markov, who also first applied them to linguistic material (1), and of C. E. Shannon, who made further fundamental contributions to the theory (2). The solution of this problem is obviously facilitated by parsing both the oral message and the language code that underlies it into discrete binary units of information as their ultimate components. As long as oral speech was assumed to be a continuum, the situation appeared "considerably more involved". (3)

1.3 If, for instance, a language such as Turkish possesses the grave flat /u/, the grave plain /ɨ/, the acute flat /y/ and the acute plain /i/, the distinction of /u/ and /i/ is optimal, since grave and flat as well as acute and plain possess a common denominator - a downward or upward shift of the formants, respectively. The combination of grave and plain or of acute and flat has no common denominator and hence is not optimal.

2.2 Further experimental work is necessary before a conclusive solution of the problem of the vocalic and consonantal features can be given. The attempt to reduce these two features to a mere difference in their respective source functions appears to us now as somewhat of an oversimplification. We tentatively suggest the following definitions of the acoustical properties of these features:

Phonemes possessing the vocalic feature are acoustically characterized by the presence of formants with small damping and hence with a relatively narrow band width. Phonemes possessing the consonantal feature are acoustically characterized by a broadening, reduction and fusion of formants and formant regions due to zeros, high damping or transient variations of formant frequencies.

On the perceptual level Stumpf defined vowels as speech sounds with distinct chromaticity (ausgeprägte Färbung) and consonants as speech sounds without distinct chromaticity. In the diffuse vowels the chromaticity and in the compact consonants the achromaticity is attenuated (cf. 2.4233). Thus the optimal contrast is presented by a compact vowel and a diffuse consonant.

2.413 and 2.4233 Through the kindness of Dr. F. S. Cooper we have received the diagram of the experiment in Haskins Laboratories and thus we may give a more exact interpretation. The "schematic stop was judged by a large majority of the subjects," to be [k] when endowed with frequencies similar to the second formant of the following vowel. Otherwise, this stop was recognized as [p] or [t] depending upon whether or not its frequencies were lower than the second formant of [i].

2.431 The French syllabic [i] and non-syllabic [i] are phonemically opposed to each other as tense /i/ and lax /i/ (cf. Reference (34), Chapter 2). The sum of the deviations of the formants of the syllabic vowel is greater than that of the corresponding non-syllabic vowel.

|  | $F_1$ | $F_2$ | $F_3$ | $\Sigma\Delta$ f |
|---|---|---|---|---|
| **Neutral Position** (G. de Saussure) | 520 | 1560 | 2600 | |
| ai /ai/ "ai" | 270 | 2000 | 3200 | |
| Δf | 250 | 440 | 600 | 1290 |
| ail /ai/ "garlic" | 410 | 1930 | 3000 | |
| Δf | 110 | 370 | 400 | 880 |

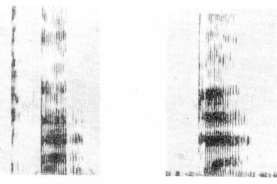

Fig. 1: Checked (glottalized) vs. unchecked consonant. Circassian: /pˀa/ "place" - /pa/ "be out of breath!" In the checked consonants the closure is abrupt and is followed by a period of silence.

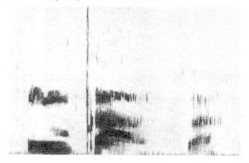

Fig. 2. Dental click. Xhosa: <u>inkcaza</u> "comb." The spectrogram clearly shows the two successive explosions (dental and velar).

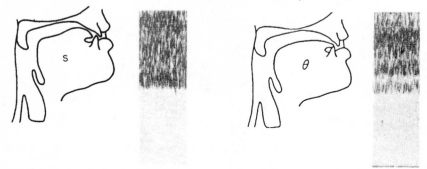

Fig. 3. Strident vs. mellow constrictives. English /s/ - /θ/. The spectrograms show the separation of formant regions in the mellow /θ/ which is not apparent in the spectrogram of the strident /s/. In the articulation profiles we can see the more complicated obstacle of strident /s/ where the air flow breaks against the edges of the lower teeth, while in the production of /θ/ the lower teeth are covered by the tongue.

- 47 -

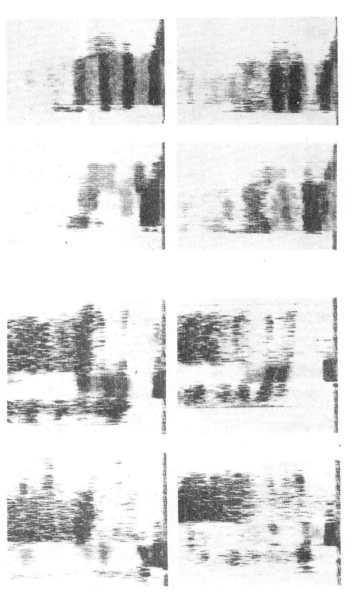

Fig. 4. The tonality features in vowels. Turkish:

/kus/ "vomit" - /kys/ "reduce"       /on/ "ten" - /øn/ "front"
/kïs/ "malevolent" - /kis/ "tumor"   /an/ "moment" - /en/ "width"

Horizontal pairs illustrate the opposition grave vs. acute. The grave member of the opposition (left) has a lower second formant. Vertical pairs illustrate the opposition of flat vs. plain. In the spectrogram of the flat member of the opposition (above), the second and third (and some higher) formants are shifted downwards.

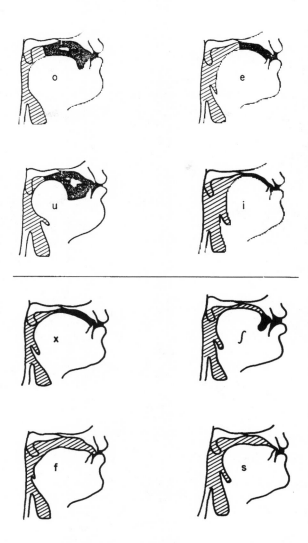

Fig. 5. Grave vs. acute and compact vs. diffuse phonemes. X-ray photographs of the production of Czech vowels and constrictives: Horizontal pairs illustrate the articulatory correlates of the opposition grave vs. acute. In the articulation of the grave member of the opposition (left), the front cavity (black area) is larger while the pharynx and lips are more contracted than in the corresponding acute (right). Vertical pairs illustrate the articulatory correlates of the opposition compact vs. diffuse. In the production of the compact phonemes (above) the ratio of the volume of the front cavity (black area) to that of the back cavity (shaded area) is higher than in the corresponding diffuse (below).

Fig. 6.  Flat (rounded) consonants. Circassian: /p̍ᵇa/ "shell". The comparison with the corresponding plain (unrounded) consonant in /p'a/ (see Fig. 1) shows the decrease in the intensity of the high frequencies and the concomitant lowering of the second formant in the following vowel despite the intervening silence.

Fig. 7:  Flat (pharyngealized) vs. plain consonants. Arabic /ṣi:n/ "China" -- /si:n/ "spelling name of letter s". The pharyngealized consonant displays energy in a lower frequency region and affects the second formant of the following vowel in a downward direction.

Fig. 8.  Flat (retroflex) vs. plain consonants. Bengali: /ṣa/ - /sa/ "spelling names of letters." The retroflex consonant has energy in a lower frequency region and affects the third formant of the following vowel in a downward direction.

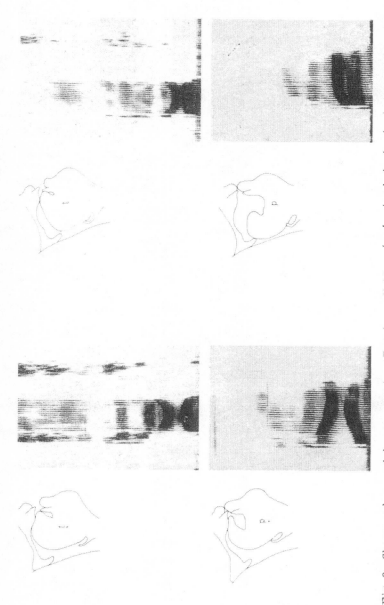

Fig. 9. Sharpened vs. plain consonants: Russian syllables /tot/ - /tot/; /pa/ - /pa/. The articulatory correlate of sharpened vs. plain consonants is a narrowing of the mouth cavity in conjunction with a widening of the pharyngeal cavity. The latter is particularly striking in the case of the grave stop /p/. The spectrograms show the higher concentration of energy in the upper frequency region of the sharpened vs. the plain consonant, as well as the characteristic rise in the second and/or third formants of the adjacent vowel.

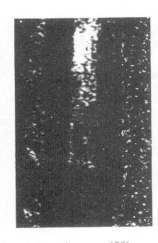

Fig. 10. Consonants in position not adjacent to vowels. Intervalgrams (33) of English whist - whisp - whisk. In /t/ the higher frequencies predominate; in /p/ the lower frequencies predominate; while in /k/ neither the upper nor the lower frequency regions predominate.

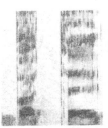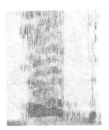

Fig. 11. Nasal and corresponding oral vowels and consonants. French bonté /bõte/ "goodness" - botter /bote/ "put on boots", Rome /rom/ "Rome" - robe /rob/ "dress".

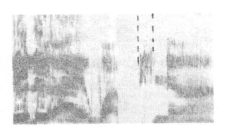

Fig. 12. Voiceless and voiced vowels. Comanche /t'írí⁷aiwapinïï/ "hired hands" - /t'ipinïï/ "stones".

# REFERENCES

PREFACE

(1) R-M. S. Heffner, General Phonetics, Madison 1949; K. L. Pike, Phonetics, Ann Arbor 1943; R. H. Stetson, Motor Phonetics, Amsterdam 1951.
(2) D. Jones, An English Pronouncing Dictionary, 7th ed., New York 1946, and An Outline of English Phonetics, 6th ed., New York 1940.
(3) "The Principles of the International Phonetic Association, being a description of the International Phonetic Alphabet and the manner of using it," Department of Phonetics, University College, London, W.C.1, 1949.
(4) "Transcription phonétique et translitération," - Propositions établies par la conférence tenue à Copenhague en Avril 1925, Oxford 1926.
(5) R. Jakobson, Sound and Meaning (to appear).

CHAPTER I

(1) D. Gabor, "Lectures on Communication Theory," Research Laboratory of Electronics, M.I.T. 1951.
(2) D. Jones, The Phoneme: Its Nature and Use, Cambridge, 1950.
(3) N. Wiener, The Human Use of Human Beings, Boston, 1950.
(4) Y. R. Chao, "The Non-Uniqueness of Phonemic Solutions of Phonetic Systems," Bulletin of the Institute of History and Philology, Academia Sinica, IV, part 4, Shanghai, 1934.
(5) N. Trubetzkoy, "Grundzüge der Phonologie," Travaux du Cercle Linguistique de Prague, VII, 1939; or the French translation by J. Cantineau, Principes de phonologie, Paris 1949.
(6) S. S. Stevens, "A Definition of Communication," J. Ac. Soc. Am., XXII, No. 6, 1950.
(7) R. M. Fano, "The Transmission of Information," M.I.T., Research Laboratory of Electronics, Technical Report, No. 65, 1949.
(8) R. Potter, "Visible Patterns of Sound," Science, 1945.
(9) B. Bloch, "A set of postulates for phonemic analysis," Language, XXIV, 1948.
(10) L. L. Beranek, Acoustic Measurements, New York 1949.
(11) R. M. Fano, "The Information Theory Point of View in Speech Communication," J. Ac. Soc. Am., XXII, No. 6, 1950.
(12) C. C. Fries and K. L. Pike, "Coexistent Phonemic Systems," Language, XXV, 1949.
(13) R. Jakobson, "On the Identification of Phonemic Entities," Travaux du Cercle Linguistique de Copenhague, V, 1949.
(14) K. Togeby, "Structure immanente de la langue française," Travaux du Cercle Linguistique de Copenhague, VI, 1951.
(15) M. Joos, "Description of Language Design," J. Ac. Soc. Am., XXII, No. 5, 1950.
(16) T. Chiba and M. Kajiyama, The Vowel, Its Nature and Structure, Tokyo, 1941; C. G. M. Fant, "Transmission Properties of the Vocal Tract," M.I.T. Acoustics Laboratory, Quarterly Progress Report, July-Septem-

ber, and October-December, 1950; H. K. Dunn, "The Calculation of Vowel Resonances, and an Electrical Vocal Tract," J. Ac. Soc. Am., XXII, No. 6, 1950.

(17) S. S. Stevens and H. Davis, Hearing, New York 1938.

(18) K. L. Pike, Tone Languages, Ann Arbor 1948.

(19) S. Smith, "Contribution to the Solution of Problems Concerning the Danish Stød," Nordisk Tidsskrift for Tale og Stemme, VIII, 1944.

(20) Z. S. Harris, Methods in Structural Linguistics, Chicago 1951.

(21) E. Sapir, "Grading: A Study in Semantics," Selected Writings, Berkeley and Los Angeles, 1949.

CHAPTER II

(1) R. K. Potter, G. A. Kopp, and H. C. Green, Visible Speech, New York 1947.

(2) E. A. Guillemin, Communication Networks, II, New York 1935; W. H. Huggins, "Conjectures Concerning the Analysis and Synthesis of Speech in Terms of Natural Frequencies," Cambridge Field Station Report, 9 February 1949.

(3) C. G. M. Fant, "Transmission Properties of the Vocal Tract," M.I.T. Acoustics Laboratory, Quarterly Progress Report, July-September 1950 and October-December 1950; "Transmission Properties of the Vocal Tract," Technical Report #12, M.I.T. Acoustics Laboratory, 1952; "Acoustic Analysis of Speech -- A Study for the Swedish Language," Ericsson Technics, 1952.

(4) C. F. Sacia and C. J. Beck, "The Power of Fundamental Speech Sounds," Bell Syst. Tech. J., V, 1926.

(5) P. Menzerath and A. de Lacerda, Koartikulation, Steuerung und Lautabgrenzung, Berlin - Bonn 1933.

(6) N. J. Jušmanov, "Phonetic Parallels between the African and the Japhetic Languages," Academy of Sciences of the USSR, Africana, I, Leningrad 1937; R. Stopa, "Die Schnalzlaute im Zusammenhang mit den sonstigen Lautarten der menschlichen Sprache," Archiv f. vergleichende Phonetik, III, 1939.

(7) E. Sapir, "Glottalized Continuants in Navaho, Nootka, and Kwakiutl," Selected Writings, Berkeley and Los Angeles, 1949.

(8) J. C. R. Licklider, "Basic Correlates of the Auditory Stimulus," Handbook of Experimental Psychology, ed. by S. S. Stevens, New York 1951.

(9) N. Trubetzkoy, "Les consonnes latérales de quelques langues caucasiques septentrionales," Bulletin de la Société de Linguistique de Paris, XXII, 1922.

(10) H. Dudley, "The Carrier Nature of Speech," Bell Syst. Tech. J. XIX, 1940.

(11) R. K. Potter and J. C. Steinberg, "Toward the Specification of Speech," J. Ac. Soc. Am., XXII, No. 6, 1950.

(12) P. Delattre, "The Physiological Interpretation of Sound Spectrograms," PMLA LXVI, No. 5, 1951.

(13) A. Sovijärvi, Die gehaltenen, geflüsterten und gesungenen Vokale und Nasale der finnischen Sprache, Helsinki 1938.

(14) H. Fletcher, Speech and Hearing, New York 1929.

(15) A. M. Liberman, P. Delattre and F. S. Cooper, "Study of One Factor in the Perception of the Unvoiced Stop Consonants," Program of the Forty-second Meeting of the Acoustical Society of America, Chicago 1951.

(16) S. S. Newman, "Further Experiments in Phonetic Symbolism," American Journal of Psychology, 1933.

(17) K. Huber, "Die Vokalmischung und das Qualitätensystem der Vokale," Archiv für Psychologie, XCI, 1934.

(18) L'Abbé Millet, Etude expérimentale de la formation des voyelles, Paris 1938.

(19) B. Polland and B. Hála, Les radiographies de l'articulation des sons tchèques, Prague 1926; B. Hála, Uvod do fonetiky, Prague 1948.

(20) W. H. Gairdner, The Phonetics of Arabic, Oxford, 1925.

(21) C. Stumpf, Die Sprachlaute, Berlin 1926.

(22) R. Jakobson "Kindersprache, Aphasie und allgemeine Lautgesetze," Språkvetenskapliga Sällskapets i Uppsala Förhandlingar, 1940-1942.

(23) D. B. Judd, "Basic Correlates of the Visual Stimulus," Handbook of Experimental Psychology, ed. by S. S. Stevens, New York 1951.

(24) P. L. Garvin, "Wichita I: Phonemics," Int. J. Am. Ling. XVI, 1950.

(25) N. Trubetzkoy, "Die Konsonantensysteme der ostkaukasischen Sprachen," Caucasica, VIII, 1931.

(26) P. - J. Rousselot, Principes de phonétique expérimentale, II, Paris 1908.

(27) D. Westermann and I. C. Ward, Practical Phonetics for Students of African Languages, London 1933.

(28) M. Joos, Acoustic Phonetics, Baltimore 1948.

(29) N. Nitsch, Z historji polskich rymów, Warsaw 1912.

(30) H. Sweet, A Primer of Phonetics, Oxford, 1906.

(31) M. Dluska, "Polskie a frykaty," Travaux du Laboratoire de phonétique expérimentale de l'Université Jean-Casimir de Léopol, II, 1937.

(32) Sokolowsky, "Zur Charakteristik der Vokale," Zeitschrift f. Hals-Nasen-und Ohrenheilkunde, VI, 1923.

(33) S. H. Chang, G. E. Pihl and J. Wiren, "The Intervalgram as a Visual Representation of Speech Sounds," J. Ac. Soc. Am. XXIII, No. 6, 1951.

(34) R. Jakobson and J. Lotz, "Notes on the French Phonemic Pattern," Word, V, 1949.


APPENDIX

(1) A. A. Markov, "Essai d'une recherche statistique sur le texte du roman 'Eugène Onĕgin', illustrant la liaison des épreuves en chaine," Bulletin de l'Académie Impériale des Sciences de St. Petersbourg, VII, 1913.

(2) C. E. Shannon, "The Redundancy of English," Cybernetics, Transactions of the Seventh Conference, ed. by H. von Foerster, New York 1951 and "Prediction and Entropy of Printed English," Bell Syst. Tech. J. XXX, 1951.

(3) C. E. Shannon and W. Weaver, The Mathematical Theory of Communication, Urbana 1949.

# SUPPLEMENT
## Tenseness and Laxness

ROMAN JAKOBSON and MORRIS HALLE

In discussing the opposition of the so-called tense and lax vowel classes, particularly the distinction between the tense /i/ and /u/ and the lax /ɪ/ and /ʊ/, Daniel Jones states that the reference to the different degrees of muscular tension on the part of the tongue is inadequate. 'A description of the English short [i] as a vowel in which the tongue is lowered and retracted from the "close" position is generally sufficiently accurate for ordinary, practical work. The term "lax" may also be used to describe the organic position of the English short [u] (in *put* /put/) as compared with the long "tense" [uː] in *boot* /buːt/). Here the organic characteristics of short [u] as compared with long [uː] might be more accurately described as a lowering and advancement of the tongue and a wider opening of the lips.'[1] This lowered and *retracted* [i] and the lowered and *advanced* [u] along with all other lax vowels, as observed by Carl Stumpf, 'shift toward the middle of the vocalic triangle'.[2] Any lax vowel 'liegt stets mehr nach der Dreiecksmitte zu' than the corresponding tense vowel (p. 262). Hence, as was noted by Gunnar Fant and ourselves[3] a tense vowel compared to its lax counterpart is produced with a greater deviation from the neutral position of the vocal tract, i.e. from the position that the vocal tract assumes in producing a very open [æ]; consequently a tense vowel displays a greater deviation from the neutral formant pattern.[4]

In the chapter 'Vowels' in his 'Handbook of Phonetics' (1877), Henry Sweet declared that 'the most important general modifications are those which cause the distinction of narrow and wide' (since renamed 'tense' and 'lax'). Sweet succeeded in demonstrating the autonomy of each of these two series 'from high to low' and the possibility of a division of any vocalic class into pairs of tense and lax vowels. In the following we shall differentiate these two series by employing the exponent [1] for tense vowels, and the exponent [2] for lax vowels, a device that has often been used in dialectology.

This autonomy of the tense-lax distinction is clearly exhibited by those African languages which display vowel harmony based on the opposition of tense and lax. Thus in Bari with its five tense and five corresponding lax vowels – /u¹/, /o¹/, /a¹/, /e¹/, /i¹/, and /u²/, /o²/, /a²/, /e²/, /i²/ – 'a word with a tense vowel in the stem will have a lax vowel in the prefix or suffix': cf. /to¹-gi¹rja¹/, *to make wipe*, and /to²-gi²rja²/, *to cause to cicatrize*.[5] Likewise in Maasai, stems consist either of tense

Written in Stanford, California, March 1961, for the Commemorative Volume to Daniel Jones (London 1962).

or of lax vowels which determine the tense or the lax character of the vowels in the affixes; moreover, in some grammatical categories, lax stem vowels alternate with the corresponding tense vowels.[6] In Ibo, with its four tense-lax pairs, namely close (diffuse) $/u^1/ - /u^2/$, $/i^1/ - /i^2/$, and open (compact) $/o^1/ - /o^2/$, $/e^1/ - /e^2/$, a peculiar interplay of the lax-tense and compact-diffuse features underlies the vowel harmony: the vowel in the verbal prefixes is diffuse before a tense root vowel, and compact, if the root vowel is lax.[7]

While Melville Bell, who first drew attention to the tense-lax distinction ascribed the decisive rôle to differences in the behaviour of the pharynx, Sweet put the chief emphasis on the 'shape of the tongue'.[8] Later investigations, however, as summed up in Heffner's *General Phonetics*, have shifted the reference 'from tongue elevations and tongue muscle tensions to laryngeal positions and air pressures'.[9]

Sievers was already aware of the fact that 'along with the lowering mouth tension also the tension of the vocal bands decreases' and 'dies macht sich praktisch in einer entsprechenden "Verdumpfung" ... des betreffenden Vocalklangs bemerkbar'.[10] Later, Meyer, in his detailed study of tense vowels, singled out the cardinal rôle of the sound-pressure: 'In dem verschiedenen Grade der Stimmbandpressung und der dadurch bedingten Verschiedenheit des durchstreichenden Atem-quantums, der 'Luftfüllung' der hervorgebrachten Laute, erblicke ich den wesentlichen Unterschied zwischen den gespannten und unges-pannten Vokalen.'[11]

The heightened subglottal air pressure in the production of tense vowels is indissolubly paired with a longer duration. As has been repeatedly stated by different observers, the tense vowels are necessarily lengthened in comparison with the corresponding lax phonemes. Tense vowels have the duration needed for the production of the most clear-cut, optimal vowels; in comparison with them the lax vowels appear as quantitatively and qualitatively *reduced*, obscured and deflected from their tense counterpart towards the neutral formant pattern.

Sweet, who generally retained Bell's terminology as 'admirably clear and concise', preferred in this instance to substitute 'narrow' for the term 'primary', which labelled the tense vowels in Bell's *Visible Speech* of 1867.[12] Sweet's terminological suggestion, however, obscured the relevant fact, so clearly expressed in Bell's nomenclature, that it is the tense vowels which constitute the 'primary', optimal vocalic pattern and that laxness represents a secondary reduction of this pattern.

There exist in language alternative ways of quantitative reduction, both observable, e.g. in the unstressed vocalic patterns; one leads from tenseness to laxness, while the other, from compactness to diffuseness. *Ceteris paribus* a diffuse (closer) vowel is shorter than the corresponding compact (opener) vowel, for example /i/, /u/ vs. /e/, /o/, whereas the lax vowel, notwithstanding its opèner articulation, displays a shorter duration than the corresponding tense vowel, as $/i^2/$, $/u^2/$, $/e^2/$, $/o^2/$ vs.

/i¹/, /u¹/, /e¹/, /o¹/. Sievers rightly warns against the deep-rooted confusion of these two distinctions: 'Man hüte sich auch davor, die Begriffe "gespannt" (oder "eng") und "ungespannt" (oder "weit") mit denen zu verwechseln, welche die althergebrachten Ausdrüke "geschlossen" und "offen" bezeichnen sollen.'[13]

The 'high-narrow' vowels are particularly short, because they are both lax and diffuse; therefore the opposition of tense/lax in the diffuse vowels may be implemented not only by such pairs as [i] – [ɪ] or [u] – [ʊ] but also by pairs syllabic vs. non-syllabic: [i] – [j] and [u] – [w]. The French vocalic pattern with its consistent opposition of tense and lax phonemes exemplifies this type of bifurcation of the diffuse vowels: the distinction [ai] /i¹/ *aï* – [aj] /ai²/ *ail* corresponds to such pairs as /te¹t/, *tête* – /te²t/, *tette*. In French, [i], like other tense vowels, displays a longer duration and a greater sum of deviations from the neutral formant pattern than the lax [j].[14]

The cardinal rôle of duration in the opposition tense/lax suggests the question of the relationship between this feature and the prosodic opposition long/short. In *Fundamentals of Language* we sought to delimit two kinds of phonemic features: 'A *prosodic* feature is displayed only by those phonemes which form the crest of the syllable and it may be defined only with reference to the relief of the syllable or of the syllabic chain, whereas the *inherent* feature is displayed by phonemes irrespective of their rôle in the relief of the syllable and the definition of such a feature does not refer to the relief of the syllable or of the syllabic chain.'[15] In Sweet's terms, quantity 'belongs essentially to the synthesis of sounds, for it is always relative, always implying comparison', particularly a comparison 'of two different sounds'.[16] The prosodic length of a vowel is inferred from the contrast of long and *ceteris paribus* short vowels in a syllabic sequence, whereas length as a component of the tenseness feature is intrinsically connected with the other, qualitative manifestations of the given feature within the same phoneme.

In his scrutiny of the Dutch phonemic pattern de Groot notes that compared with their tense counterparts, the lax vowels are not only duller and slacker but also shorter ('ceteris paribus immer kürzer'), yet for the identification of these phonemes shortness is hardly decisive, since however much one stretches /a²/ in /rá²t/, *rad*, 'wheel', it does not change into /rá¹t/, *raad*, 'council'. Thus despite a close interrelation and manifold convertibility between the inherent feature tense/lax and the prosodic feature long/short, these features belong to two substantially different kinds of distinctive features.

The attentive analysis of the tense/lax feature discloses, however, an identical tripartition of each of the two classes. The three types of prosodic feature which, following Sweet, we have termed *tone, force*, and *quantity*, and which correspond to the main attributes of sound sensation – pitch, loudness, and perceptual duration, find a close analogue in the three types of inherent feature. The 'tonality' and 'sonority' features, which we attempted to outline in *Fundamentals* (§ 3.6), are akin to the prosodic features of tone and force. The tense/lax opposition should, however, be detached from the sonority features and viewed as a separate, 'protensity' feature, which among the inherent features corresponds to the quantity features in the prosodic field.

The neutralization of the pharynx in the production of lax vowels (its contraction and correspondingly the somewhat lowered tonality in the front series of lax vowels and a pharyngeal dilatation with a heightened tonality in the back series) reveals a certain similarity with the formation and structure of the centralized vowels in a few Nilotic, Caucasian, and Hindu languages. Their vocalism seems to present a peculiar implementation of the phonemic opposition tense/lax, and correspondingly such a system as that of Dinka would have to be viewed as composed of seven pairs: $/u^1/$ [u] – $/u^2/$ [ĭ], $/o^1/$ [o] – $/o^2/$ [ö], $/ɔ^1/$ [ɔ] – $/ɔ^2/$ [ö̆], $/a^1/$ [a] – $/a^2/$ [ä], $/\varepsilon^1/$ [ɛ] – $/\varepsilon^2/$ [ë], $/e^1/$ [e] – $/e^2/$ [ë], $/i^1/$ [i] – $/i^2/$ [ɪ].[18] This question, however, requires further investigation.

In analysing the phonemic pattern of Dutch, de Groot tentatively identified the relation between the tense and lax vowels with the consonantal opposition of the fortes and lenes.[19] The common denominator of both relations is now apparent. Fortes are always opposed to lenes by a higher air pressure behind the point of articulation and by a longer duration. This difference may be accompanied by the voicelessness of the fortes and the voicing of the lenes or may lack such concomitant cues. A typical example of tense and lax stops and fricatives, all of them produced without any participation of voice, is provided by the Swiss German consonantal pattern. As its first investigator Winteler stated, the distinctive mark in a fortis-lenis pair is 'das Mass der auf die Bildung der Laute verwendeten Expirations- und Artikulations-energie oder deutlicher, die Empfindung von der Stärke des Expirationsdruckes und des davon abhängigen Widerstandes der artikulierenden Organe, sowie das Mass der Dauer der beiderlei Laute'.[20] This outstanding forerunner of modern phonology precisely defined the essence of the fortis-lenis opposition: 'Bei der Bildung der Fortes verharren die Sprachwerkzeuge fühlbar in ihrer Kulminationsstellung', whereas 'diejenigen Artikulationen, welche Lenes erzeugen, in demselben Augenblicke wieder aufgegeben werden, in welchem sie ihre Kulmination erreicht haben'.[21]

The relative duration of the consonant and the antecedent phoneme may remain for certain contextual or optional variants of tense and lax consonants the chief or even the only cue to their distinction.[22]

In sum, the production of lax as opposed to tense phonemes involves a lower (vs. higher) air pressure in the cavity behind the only or main source (i.e. below the vocal cords for the vowels, and behind the point of articulation for the consonants). Furthermore, tense phonemes are produced with more deviation from the neutral, central position than the corresponding lax phonemes: the tense consonants show primarily a longer time interval spent in a position away from neutral, while the tense vowels not only persevere in such a position optimal for the effectuation of a steady, unfolded, unreduced sound but also display a greater deformation in the vocal tract.[23]

## Notes

[1] Daniel Jones, *An Outline of English Phonetics*, 8th Ed., Cambridge, 1956, 39.

[2] Carl Stumpf, *Die Sprachlaute*, Berlin, 1926, 259.

[3] R. Jakobson, C. G. M. Fant, and M. Halle, *Preliminaries to Speech Analysis* 2nd Ed., Cambridge, Mass., May 1952, 2.43.

[4] G. Fant, *Acoustic Theory of Speech Production*, 's Gravenhage, 1960, 210.

[5] D. Westermann and I. C. Ward, *Practical Phonetics for Students of African Languages*, Oxford, 1933, 388.

[6] A. N. Tucker and J. Tompo Ole Mpaayei, *A Maasai Grammar*, London, 1955, 260.

[7] I. C. Ward, *An Introduction to the Ibo Language*, Cambridge, 1936.

[8] *Handbook*, 26 ff.

[9] R-M. S. Heffner, *General Phonetics*, Madison, Wis., 1949, 96 ff.

[10] E. Sievers, *Grundzüge der Phonetik*, 5th Ed., Leipzig, 1901, § 256.

[11] E. A. Meyer, *Festschrift Wilhelm Viëtor*, Marburg, 1910, 238.

[12] *Handbook*, XI.

[13] *Grundzüge*, § 258.

[14] Cf. the numerical data in our *Preliminaries*, 36, 46.

[15] Jakobson and Halle, *The Fundamentals of Language*, 's Gravenhage, 1956, 22.

[16] *Handbook*, § 179.

[17] A. W. de Groot, *Donum Natalicium Schrijnen*, Nijmegen-Utrecht, 1929, 549 ff.

[18] Westermann and Ward, *Practical Phonetics*, 207 ff.

[19] de Groot, *Donum*, 549 ff.

[20] J. Winteler, *Die Kerenzer Mundart des Kantons Glarus in ihren Grundzügen dargestellt*, Leipzig-Heidelberg, 1876, 25.

[21] Op cit., 27.

[22] Cf. Jones, *The Phoneme*, Cambridge, 1950, 52 ff.; F. Falc'hun, *Le système consonantique du Breton*, Part I, Rennes, 1951; P. Denes, 'The Effect of Duration on the Perception of Voicing', *J. Acoust. Soc. Amer.*, XXVII, 1955, 761 ff.; P. Martens, 'Einige Fälle von sprachlich relevanter Konsonanten Dauer im Neuhochdeutschen', *Maître Phonétique*, CIII, 1955, 5 ff.; N. Chomsky, Review of Jakobson and Halle, 'The Fundamentals of Language', *Int. J. Am. Ling.*, XXIII, 1957, 238.

[23] Fant, *Acoustic Theory*, 224 ff.

# INDEX OF TERMS